Being a Painter

BEING A PAINTER

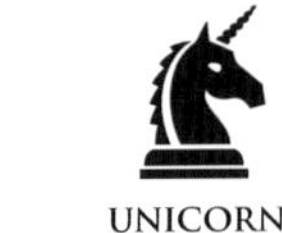
UNICORN

THE ART OF XIE SHAN

Joshua Gong

Published in 2024 by Unicorn,
an imprint of Unicorn Publishing Group
Charleston Studio
Meadow Business Centre
Lewes BN8 5RW
www.unicornpublishing.org

ISBN 978-1-916846-29-6

10 9 8 7 6 5 4 3 2 1

Designed by XYCO.UK
Printed in Turkey by FineTone Ltd

Le vent se lève !...
Il faut tenter de vivre !

The wind is rising !...
We must try to live !

Le Cimetière Marin
The Graveyard by the Sea
(1920)

by Paul Valéry

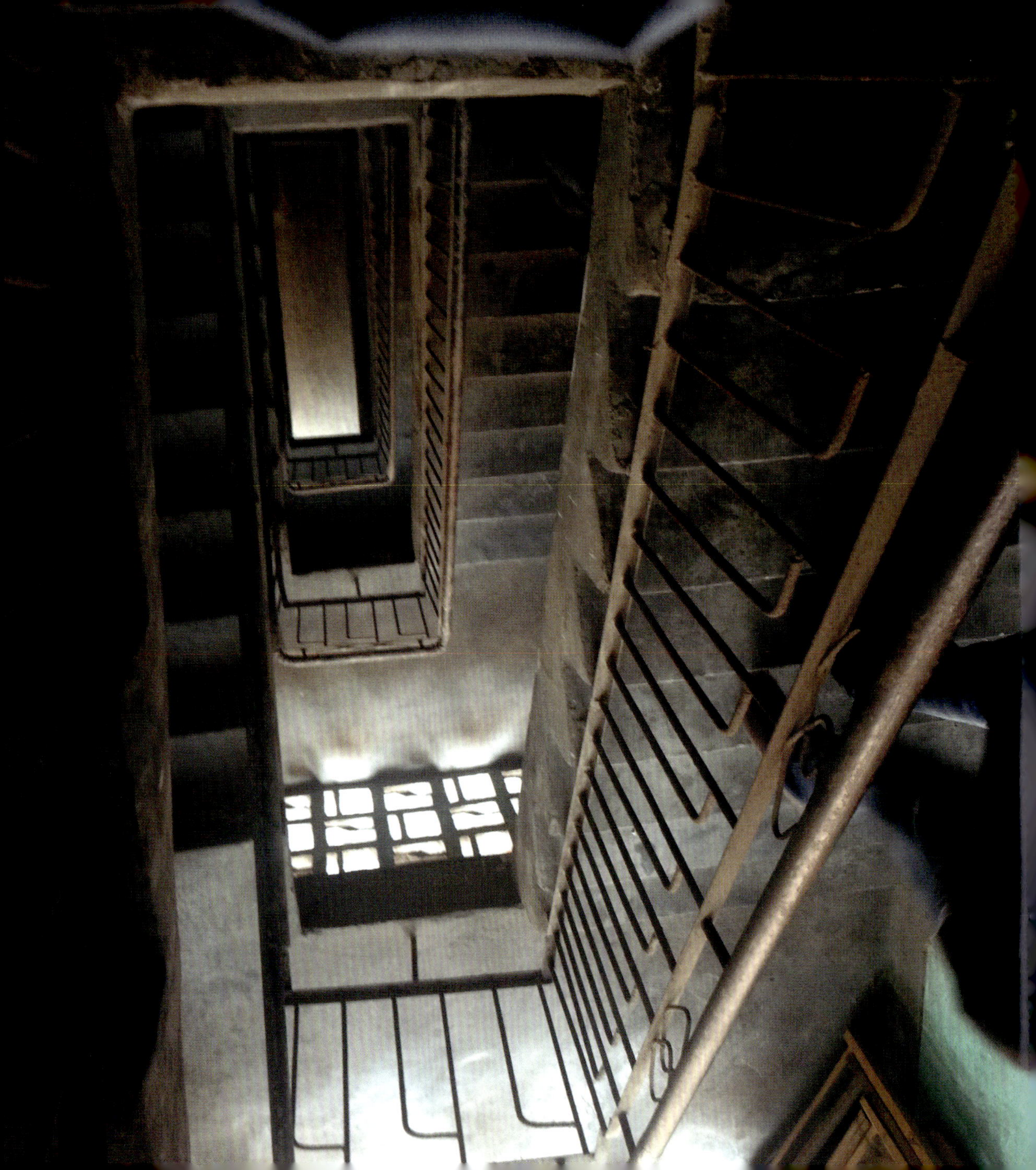

Under strong winds,
one can know the strength of grass.

The History of The Eastern Han Dynasty
(2nd Century)

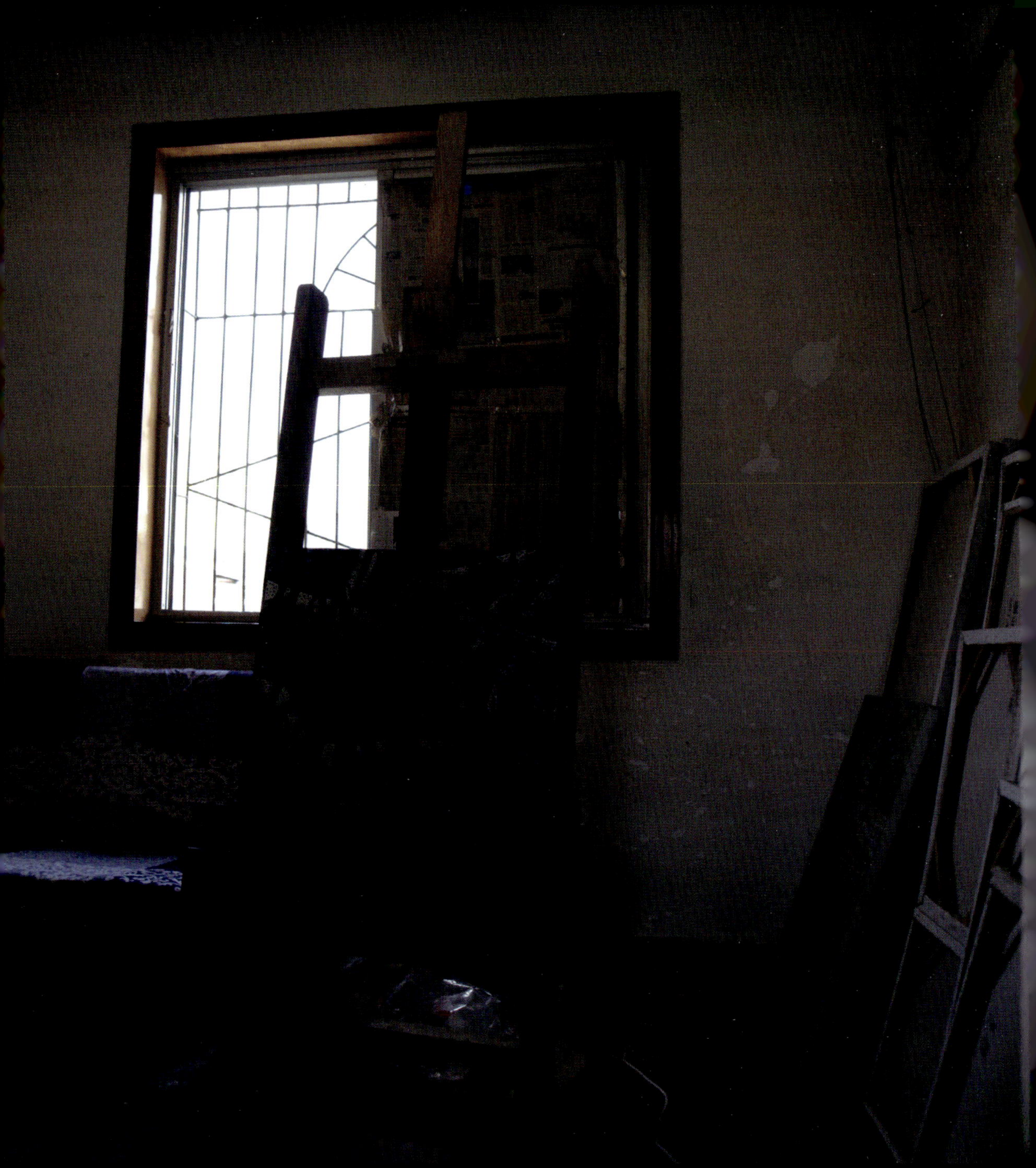

Table of Contents

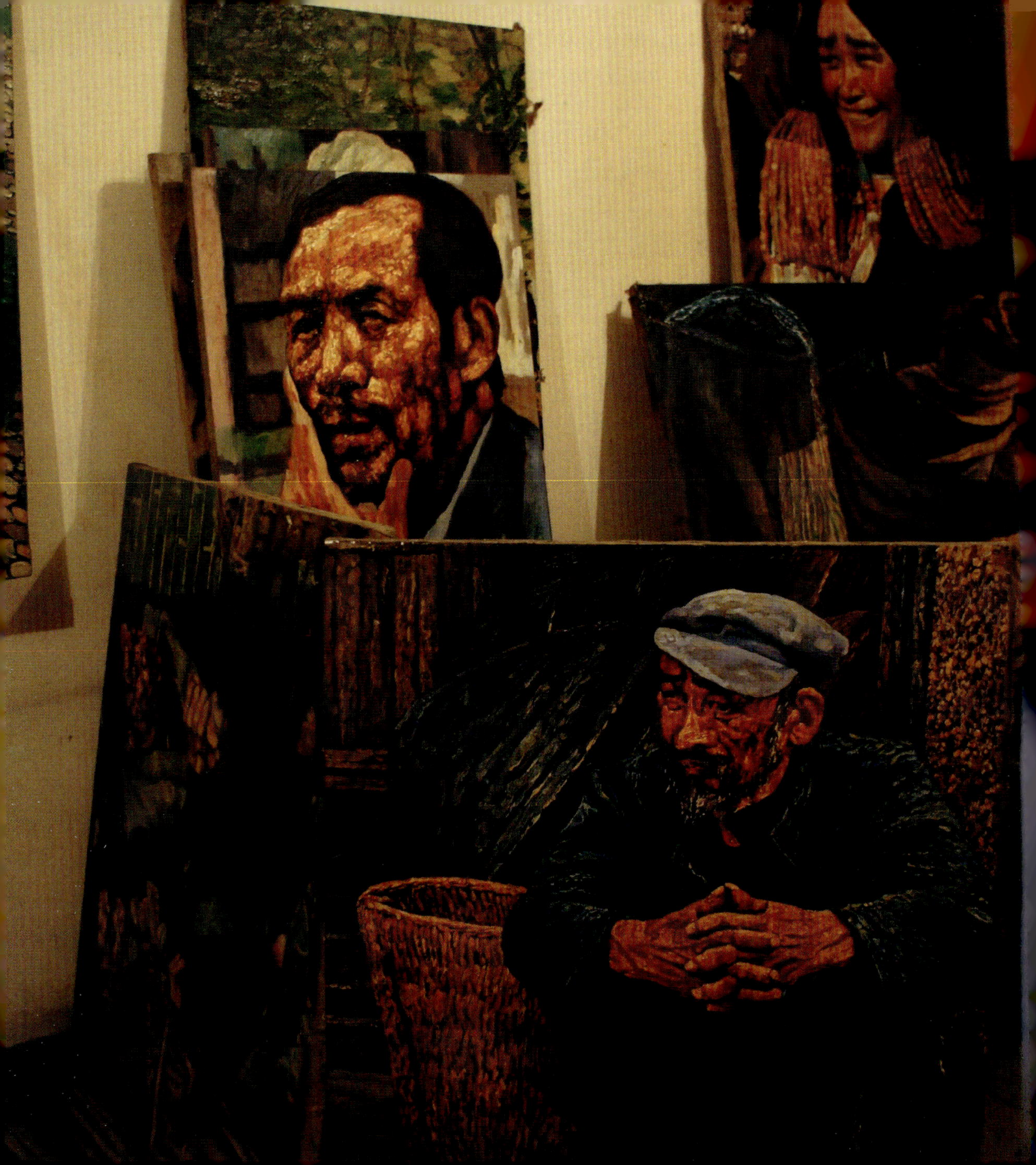

Introduction

The book portrays the journey of artist Xie Shan, who dedicated his life to painting despite suffering from cornea thinning (keratoconus), auditory hallucinations and congenital schizophrenia. As a self-taught artist, Xie Shan's exploration was purely based on visual experience. As a result of a rare sight condition and a cornea transplant in his early 20s, he attempted to capture subject matter with brilliant colour and extraordinary plasticity on canvas. Xie Shan had a challenging career path but remained resilient and persisted through the difficulties. His art style and sensibility go against the conventions of the modern art world, making his work original and unique, The book's visual and narrative potential make it a contemporary revelation of the myth of being a painter.

Chapter One: What Does It Mean to Be a Painter?

> *"There really is no such thing as Art. There are only artists."*
>
> — E.H. Gombrich[1]

Every painter embarks on a unique journey, just as every style of painting differs distinctly. The story of Xie Shan – pursuing the ideal of becoming a painter, seeking to realise his own worth while overcoming substantial obstacles from visual impairment and mental illness – is told with sincerity, specificity and simplicity. Though Xie Shan originates from a remote corner of southwest China, his story possesses a universal appeal. When discussing art, it is common for artists to be fictionalised by narrators with particular agendas who will often skew their stories with biases and dress them in

1. E.H. Gombrich, 1996, *The Essential Gombrich*, London: Phaidon, p. 65

specific cultural or symbolic masks.

In this narrative, however, the author seeks to relay a truthful account. The author acknowledges that he lacks a mystical 'reality distortion field' like that famously attributed to Steve Jobs. Telling Xie Shan's story serves as a literary method to help readers comprehend his approach to artistic creation. The guiding principles of this book are its authenticity, which lends it charm, and its artistic nature, which highlights the human condition.

From his early years, Xie Shan has been passionate about painting. He has devoted his entire life to this craft. He does not aspire to fame or rely on motivational rhetoric about success[2] to stake his life on a high-risk gamble. For Xie Shan, becoming a painter is a profound belief, a pathway to realising his self-worth. This realisation is not motivated by materialistic or utilitarian desires.[3] He does not pursue material wealth through his artwork, nor does he seek the acclaim associated with being a master artist. He purely expresses himself through his art, neither courting patrons with subservience nor showing contempt for the powerful – unlike the cynical ancient sages. He does not attempt to transcend himself and his values as Nietzsche's Übermensch might, because the pure joy derived from painting makes worldly honours seem trivial. Xie Shan's life has been marked by adversity; he has experienced numerous physical and psychological challenges on his journey to becoming a painter. Nevertheless, he has dedicated himself to painting, channelling the hardships of life into vibrant, colourful expressions of joy through his art. This joy is not overly sweet but a complex blend of bitterness and relentless perseverance.

His early works, the *Forest Series* (《树林系列》2002.002) from February 2002, encapsulate this life philosophy and creative spirit. In these paintings, a peaceful forest scene with lawns and red brick houses creates a serene pastoral mood within a natural setting. In a backdrop of refreshing green, sturdy dark-brown branches underpin the foliage. Foreground branches, painted with dynamic strokes in a lighter brown, convey the lively vitality

2. Self-help from the West was repackaged as 'success studies' in China.

3. Jeremy Bentham's utilitarianism and the theory of secular hedonism as the greatest good are, of course, open to debate.

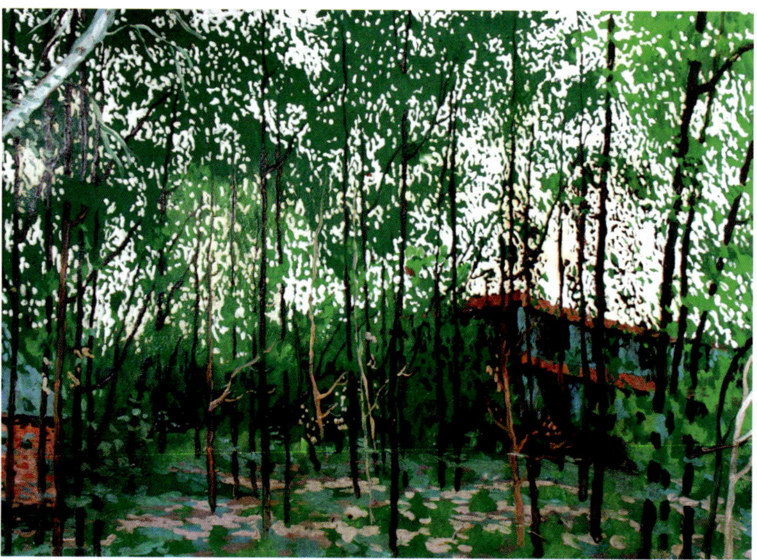

Forest Series 树林系列
2002, Oil on canvas, 40 x 60 cm

of the trees, as if they are animated by the sunlight. Between the leaves in the painting's upper reaches, sunlight peeks through. Xie Shan uses lines to evoke the delicate forms of silkworm larvae, capturing a dynamic sense born of the intense sunlight impacting the painter's vision. The composition's upper and lower segments respond to each other – one dynamic, the other serene – bringing a vibrant sense of spring to the scene. This visual experience and effect likely stem from the artist's periodic observations. Immersed in the spring sunlight, the painter's vision is fully ignited by the light filtering through the trees. Due to visual fatigue, the painter occasionally needs to close his eyes for brief respites. Upon closing his eyes, he perceives dynamic changes of red, interspersed with flashes of blue and

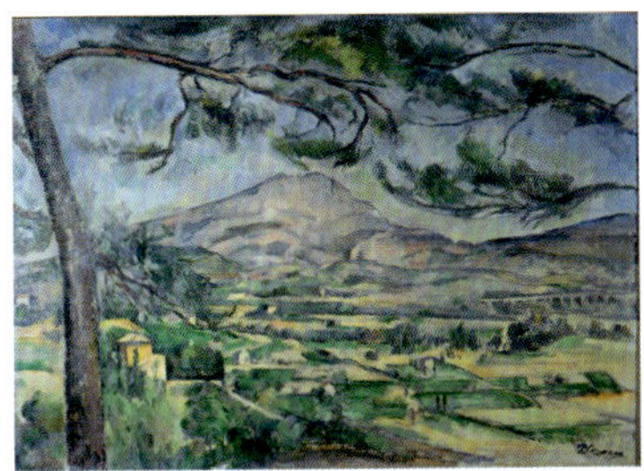

Mont Sainte-Victoire with Large Pine
Paul Cézanne
c. 1887, Oil on canvas, 67 x 92 cm
Courtauld Institute of Art, London, UK

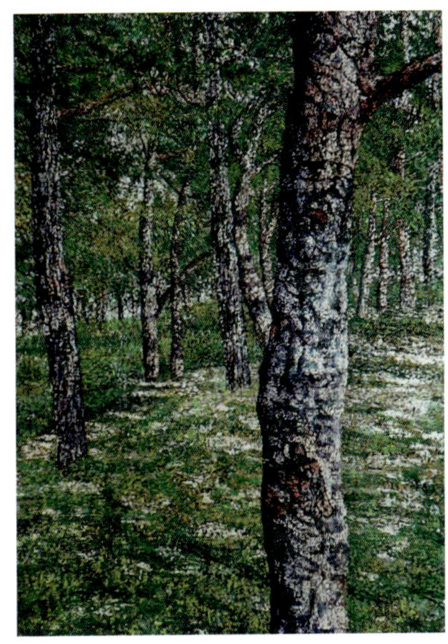

Forest No.3 树林-3
2005, Oil on canvas, 40 x 60 cm

orange. The red represents the colours seen from the sunlight illuminating the blood vessels in the eyelids, while the blue and orange could be shadows from the movements of the eyeballs and the circulation within the blood vessels. When the painter reopens his eyes, the colours previously seen with eyes closed merge with the current vista, creating a new image pulsing vibrantly with visual rhythms. These unique, flare-like patches of colour and patterns of light are subtly, or overtly, magnified by the artist; they permeate Xie Shan's body of work. This method not only facilitates his communication with the world, but it also shapes the evolution of his unique painterly style.

In *Forest No.3* (《树林-3》) (2005.001), Xie Shan revisits this pointillist technique of flare effects. In this particular work, his strokes are refined, adeptly highlighting the subtle shifts in refracted light and effectively

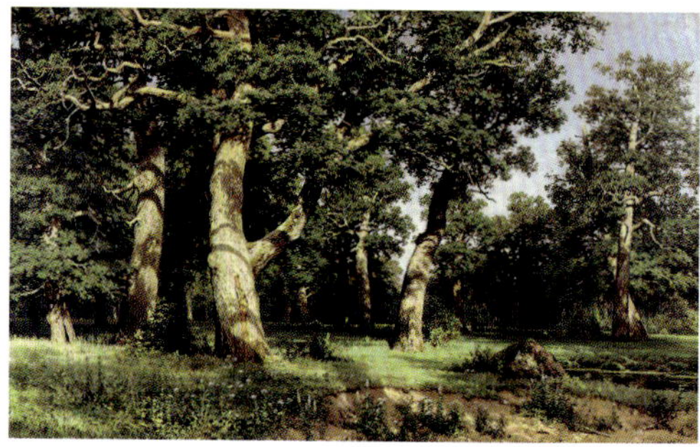

Oak Grove
Ivan Shishkin , 1887, Oil on canvas, 125 x 193 cm
Kyiv National Picture Gallery, Kyiv, Ukraine

capturing the texture of tree bark. The composition of *Forest No.3* (《树林-3》) echoes the genius found in Cézanne's *La Montagne Sainte-Victoire* series. Xie Shan uses vertical tree trunks and diagonally strewn grass to create a layered depth on an otherwise flat canvas, establishing a distinct painterly hierarchy. Although Xie Shan generally adopts a detailed, realistic approach akin to the plein air methods of the Russian Peredvizhniki and French impressionists, he also imbues his work with a personal interpretation of trees, portraying their unique natural essence. Ivan Shishkin (Иван Иванович Шишкин, 1832–98) of the Russian Peredvizhniki movement – renowned for his landscape art, particularly forest scenes – stands out for his distinctive portrayal of this theme. Xie Shan's earliest practices often involved reproducing the works of Ivan Shishkin. Through relentless copying and direct observation, Xie Shan dissected Shishkin's pictorial language. In his 1983 pen sketches that mimic Shishkin, Xie Shan refined the interplay of light and dark, using pale blue to accentuate certain highlights. The tones and shapes of these highlights served as the foundational brushwork techniques for the *Forest Series* (《树林系列》).

While Xie Shan's self-taught painting drew primarily from Western classics, the depiction of trees in his work echoes ancient Chinese art and calligraphy, which often employs landscapes to convey emotions or human characteristics symbolically. *Six Gentlemen* (《六君子图》) by Ni Zan, preserved in the Shanghai Museum, exemplifies this with ink-rendered trees metaphorically reflecting the noble virtues of ancient Chinese literati. In this artwork, Ni Zan represents the personalities of six gentlemen through six distinct types of trees. The atmospheric mists typical of Southern landscapes are vividly captured using the ink medium. Similarly, Xie Shan's *Forest No.3* (《树林-3》) portrays Southern woodlands, yet it differs by offering a closer, more detailed view, much like a close-up shot. Utilising the distinctive properties of oil paint, Xie Shan further explores the dynamic interaction between sunlight and trees, rendering the organic life with enhanced vitality and immediacy. Xie Shan's use of green captures exquisitely the ethereal mist of Southern landscapes. His paintings deftly intertwine the damp earthiness with the vibrant breath of sunlight, employing variations in brushstrokes to skilfully create a depth of space extending from the foreground to the background.

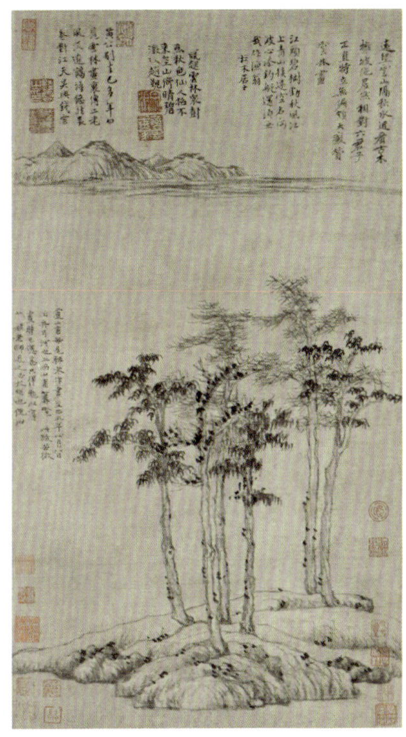

Six Gentlemen 六君子图
Ni Zan,
1345, Ink on paper mounted on haning scroll,
33.3 x 61.9 cm
Shanghai Museum, Shanghai, China

From a spiritual and temperamental perspective, Xie Shan's works underscore the inclusiveness of contemporary society towards the individual. In ancient China, particularly post–Tang dynasty, painters were evaluated against literary standards. Professional

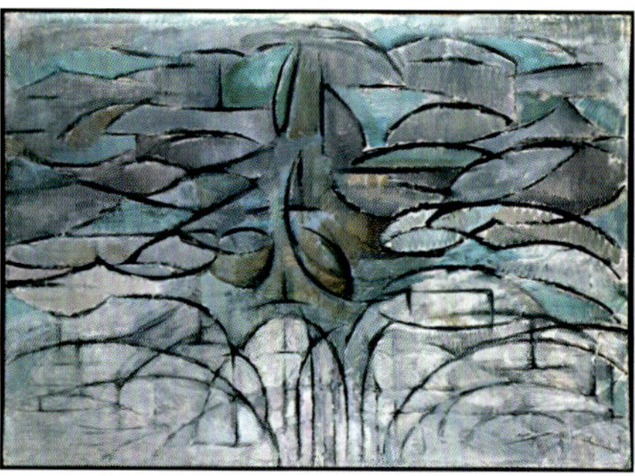

Apple Tree in Flower
Piet Mondrian
1912, Oil on canvas, 78.5 x 107.5 cm
Gemeentemuseum, The Hague, Netherlands
DeAgostini Picture Library/Scala, Florence

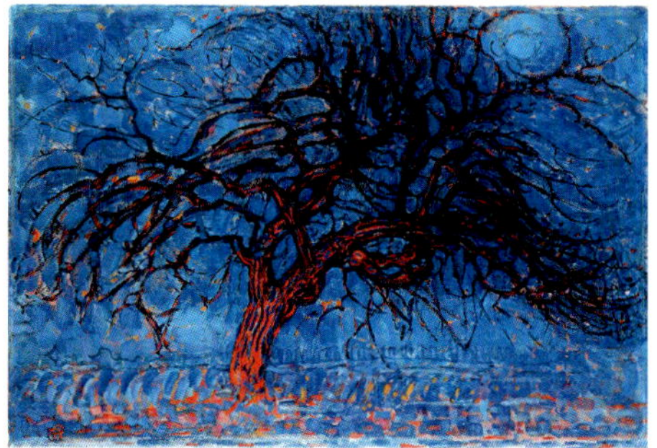

Avond (Evening); The Red Tree
Piet Mondrian
1908–10, Oil on canvas, 70 x 99 cm
Gemeente Museum, The Hague, Netherlands
DeAgostini Picture Library/Scala, Florence

painters, who earned their livelihoods through their art and its commercial aspects, were often regarded negatively, as liabilities. In the West, especially after the seventeenth century, painters were constrained by academic norms, compelled to follow classical principles and produce large-scale narrative works such as religious and historical paintings to be considered serious artists. In contemporary times, artists have far greater freedom in their choice of subjects, techniques and mediums, allowing them to explore and express visual diversity in various ways. Xie Shan's *Tree Series* evolved to become more vibrant and colourful, breaking away from traditional constraints focused on object characteristics. This transformation reflects the freedom contemporary society has afforded him in his self-directed learning and artistic creation. Xie Shan's *Colorful Leaves* (《斑斓的树叶》) (2017.002) marks a transition from Expressionism towards a style characterised by organic geometric colour blocks, reminiscent of Piet Mondrian's tree series. *Colorful Leaves* (《斑斓的树叶》) signifies Xie Shan's transition from focusing on the painterly qualities of trees to embracing an organic style of painting. He masterfully transforms the interplay of warm and cool tones into meticulously arranged colour blocks, which he scatters across the canvas

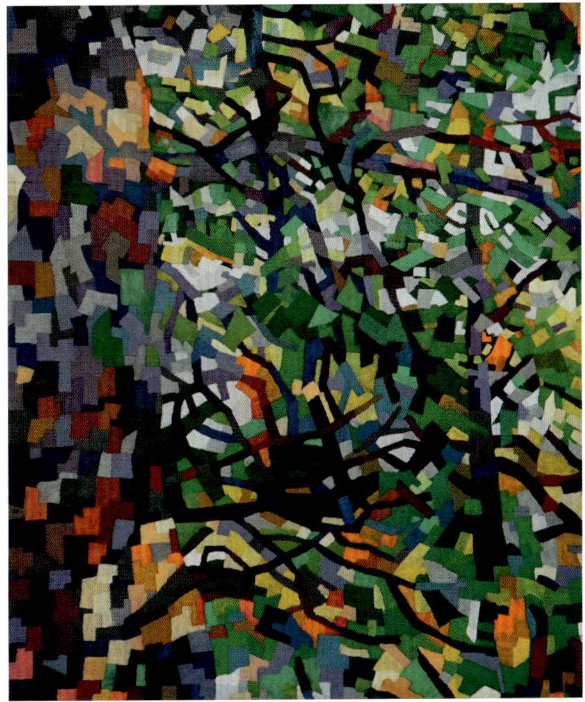

Colorful Leaves 斑斓的树叶
2017, Oil on canvas, 100 x 80 cm

with a liberal hand. The edges of these colour blocks vary, yet the overall effect avoids being mechanical or disorderly. It simultaneously retains a richness in expression and the sophistication of painting. This showcases his maturing approach in both the conceptualisation and execution of his artwork.

While Xie Shan often draws on the experiences of plein air painters and conducts thorough studies of various scenes, he maintains traditional academic practices. He refines his creations indoors, seldom completing his paintings in the field; rather, he prefers to develop the images in his mind and then render them on canvas. In a manner akin to ancient Chinese landscape painters, his creative process distinguishes between sketching in nature and painterly creation in the studio. The resulting works are visual expressions of imagination not constrained by any external appearances. Unlike freehand painters, who evoke a mystical and transcendent aesthetic, Xie Shan's artistic realm is down-to-earth yet far from ordinary; he seeks to enrich life through his art, inspiring both painters and viewers to find their personal points of connection within his paintings.

Xie Shan encountered numerous challenges from a young age. Shortly after becoming an adult, he was diagnosed with keratoconus, a degenerative condition that causes the corneas to thin and bulge into a conical shape, distorting vision and eventually leading to blindness. For Xie Shan, who had been enchanted by painting since childhood, this diagnosis was a devastating blow. He believed he would have to bid farewell to painting, which was his sole refuge and passion. However, a ray of hope emerged with a corneal transplant that partially restored his vision, thus enabling him to resume his pursuit of painting. Unfortunately, the transplant led to a severe rejection reaction, requiring intensive steroid treatments that had the effect of drastically altering his once-slender figure. He became unrecognisably large. Driven by formidable resilience, he committed to walking ten kilometres daily from his home to his studio. After more than a year of unwavering dedication, Xie Shan managed to shed nearly thirty kilograms, thus reclaiming his former shape.

Do not assume that life's hardships will easily fade away; greater misfortunes often follow in quick succession. For a while, Xie Shan became increasingly withdrawn. He confined himself to his room every day, where he focused solely on one thing: painting. He withdrew from interactions with family and classmates. His family left his meals at his door; he would eat when he was hungry and then place the empty dishes outside the door. This routine persisted, day in and day out. Then one night, he impulsively jumped from the balcony of his three-story home, driven not by a wish to end his life but by paranoid delusions. The fall broke his right leg, and he was eventually hospitalised for schizophrenia.

Xie Shan's life has been marked by severe trials, yet amidst these misfortunes there were fortunate turns. After spending over a year in the hospital, he was finally able to return home. Back in the nurturing presence of his family, he picked up his brush once more and resumed his distinctive life as a painter. However, his life remains challenging. He takes antipsychotic medication and must cope with the various side effects – intolerable for most people – that the drugs inflict on his body. He endures a day, or even longer, of debilitating side effects after each weekly dose of medication. Yet, through this all, Xie Shan has grown ever more resilient and has never forsaken his passion for painting. His artistic expression and style have faced several critical junctures, shaped by his experiences and opportunities. Each evolution has allowed him to develop a unique, original mode of communication with the outside world.

An artist's tumultuous life, including enforced separations from the artistic journey and its creations, would be a perfect premise for a novel. Biographies of artists are the prevalent form of narration in the history of art. The early Chinese text on painting history *Famous Paintings Through the Ages* (《历代名画记》) spans ten volumes, seven of which are devoted to discussing the lives of painters, thus illustrating the importance of biographies. *Famous Paintings Through the Ages* (《历代名画记》) emphasises the importance of painting for its ability to educate, assist in social relationships, explore divine transformations and probe the subtler realms. Painters are considered sages and skilled craftsmen ('There is never a lack of the wise'; 'Craftsmen of wisdom appear'), and their contributions to art history demand respect and documentation. How true is the lament that 'Since ancient times, countless acts of loyalty, filial piety, righteousness, and bravery have gone unrecorded. How much more so for the art of painting?'[4] Similarly, Giorgio Vasari's *Lives of the Most Excellent Painters, Sculptors, and Architects* from the Renaissance explicitly adopted a biographical narrative. It aligned artists' metaphorical

4. Zhang Yanyuan, *Famous Paintings through the Ages*, Tang Dynasty, https://zh.wikisource.org/wiki/歷代名畫記/卷第一 (accessed 25 Feb 2024).

life stages (birth, maturity, death, rebirth) with their historical journeys to emphasise the unique value of the art and artists of that era.[5] In discussions about artists, both in China and internationally, their art unquestionably remains the central focus. Though art historian Ernst Gombrich argued that the artist should be considered before the art, discussing an artist without addressing the achievements of their work is like missing the forest for the trees. W. Somerset Maugham's character Strickland, inspired by Gauguin, exemplifies the vast difference between fictional characters and real artists; exploring that difference is akin to comparing the moon to sixpence.

Reserved yet confident in his painting:

Xie Shan's art is indispensable to his identity as a painter. His unique visual experiences render his paintings distinctly compelling. Since Cézanne, modern Western art has broken away from traditional constraints on painting language, thus freeing artists from the limitations imposed by the physical characteristics of their subjects. The canvas has transformed into a visual field where imagination can roam freely. In China, since the economic reforms, the prescriptive academism that had until then dictated painting content has been overturned, allowing postmodernism and modernism to develop in a rich interplay. Xie Shan draws his subjects from his life experiences, and when transforming these into art, he always remains mindful that he is primarily working within the medium of painting. He ensures his work retains a strong sense of painterliness without drifting into complete abstraction. Although his techniques are grounded in Western oil painting, the essence of his work retains an introspective spirituality with echoes of Eastern Zen.

For example, his recent pieces *Warrior by the River* (《河边的武士》) (2023.001) and *Warrior Entering the Palace* (《进入宫殿的武士》) (2022.004) might initially suggest the surreal compositions and emotional tones of

5. *Art History and Its Methods: A Critical Anthology*, 1995, ed. by Eric Fernie, London: Phaidon, pp. 22–28.

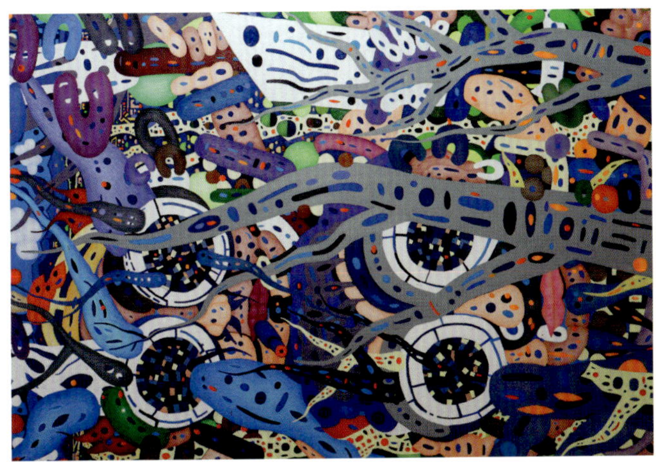

Warrior by the River 河边的武士
2023, Oil on canvas, 100 x 150 cm

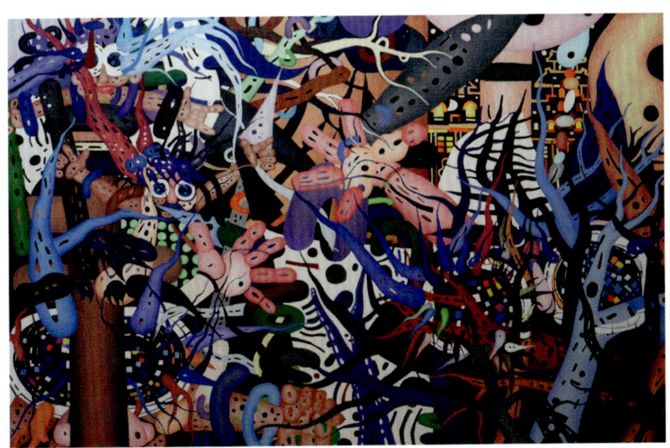

Warrior Entering the Palace 进入宫殿的武士
2022, Oil on canvas, 100 x 150 cm

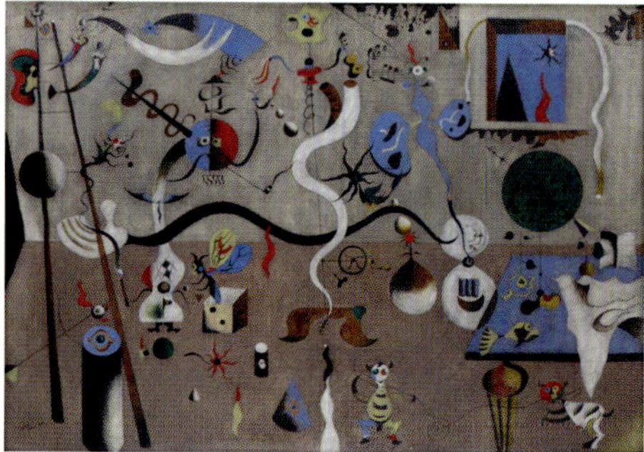

Carnival of Harlequin
Joan Miró, 1924–5, Oil on canvas, 66 x 93 cm *Buffalo AKG Art Museum, New York, USA*
© Successió Miró
ADAGP, Paris and DACS London 2024

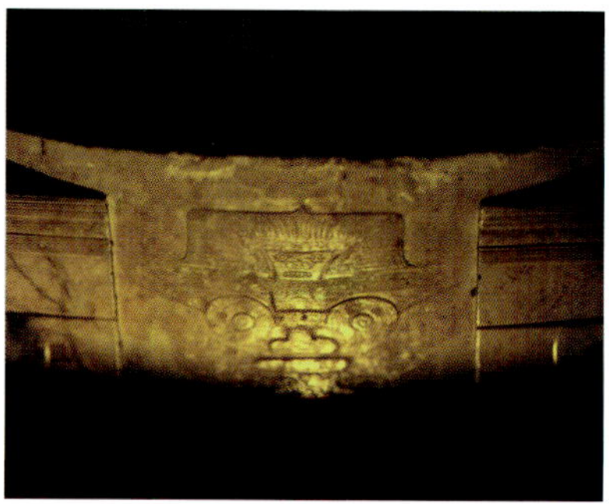

Jade, Liangzhu Culture
良渚遗址反山12号墓出土玉琮
3300-2300 BC
Photo courtesy: ©Wen Yadi

Joan Miró. However, Xie Shan's images do not aim to create a surreal, absurd theatre. He follows the traditional Chinese painting principle stated by Tang dynasty painter Zhang Zao: 'External teacher is nature, internal source is the heart.'[6] Through extensive real-life observation and thoughtful construction, he meticulously reconstructs on canvas the scenes envisaged in his mind, refining continuously to achieve a mature balance of elements during the creative process. In *Warrior by the River* (《河边的武士》), the fluid imagery is deftly arranged, with two figures, identifiable by their facial features, interwoven among depictions of branches. In his paintings, Xie Shan eschews the subconscious improvisation typical of surrealism; rather, he leverages his conscious visual experience and expertise to meticulously structure the composition, focusing on harmonising detail and the overall unity through his brushwork and techniques. In *Art and Illusion*, Ernst Gombrich highlights this approach: 'The artist who wants to "represent" a real (or imagined) thing does not start by opening his eyes and looking about

6. Zhang Yanyuan, *Famous Paintings through the Ages*, Tang Dynasty, https://zh.wikisource.org/wiki/歷代名畫記/卷第一, (accessed 27 Feb 2024).

him but by taking colours and forms and building up the required image.'[7]

Xie Shan's self-awareness is manifested through his acknowledgement of his visual sensitivity within his artwork. In *Warrior by the River* (《河边的武士》), the depiction of two sets of the painter's eyes conveys his exploration of dual perspectives. The pupils are composed of kaleidoscopic colour blocks, while the whites feature wheel-like structures, layered with multiple symbolic implications. The scene before the painter flows with images reminiscent of cellular organisms, reflecting the painter's intent to capture the microscopic vitality of life by the river. By enlarging and treating cellular shapes in blocks, the spatial depth of various plants and animals along the riverbank is effectively compressed. Branches, fruits and eyes – distinct biological elements – are seamlessly integrated through a unified visual treatment. The painter's visual consciousness begins with the eyes, which, through their perspective, are transformed by the brain's imagination into a narrative with open-ended significance. The artist, drawing from his observations and experience, uses his hands and brush to transmit visionary spaces from his mind to the canvas. This approach resonates with the creation of human- and animal-faced motifs on jade *cong* from China's ancient Liangzhu culture. Interestingly, Xie Shan was initially unaware of these ancient religious art forms, yet there exists a similarity in their creative practices. The seemingly naive images on his canvas, in reality, convey symbolic meanings that are far more complex than many realistic paintings created using the single-point perspective formula. Xie Shan's intent to affirm his identity as a painter is unmistakably evident in his work. The elements in his paintings – circles, arcs and lines – straddle the line between abstraction and representation. Through Xie Shan's personal arrangement, these initially insignificant images gain profound significance. These interpretations are not merely a straightforward 'image-to-narrative' match; they interact, allowing the static images to convey diverse perceptions through a distinctive artistic method. This practice, where visual intuition precedes conceptual thought and the language of painting is refined through discipline, epitomises the true

7. E. H. Gombrich, 1961, *Art and Illusion: A Study in the Psychology of Pictorial Representation*, 2nd Edition, London: Phaidon, p. 314.

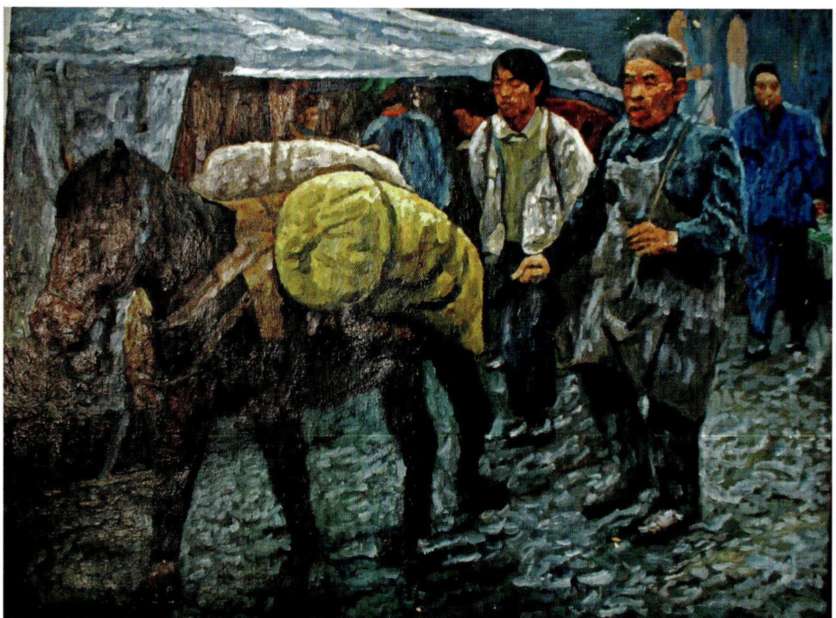

Memories of Dongxi 东溪回忆
2004, Oil on canvas,100 x 120 cm

allure of Xie Shan's art.

His unwavering commitment to artistic creation; his belief in moulding imagery; and his humility towards everything beyond his life as an artist empower him to continually refine his abilities and solidify his capabilities as a painter. His early works, infused with a rustic style and rustic themes, mirror the solemnity Vincent van Gogh demonstrated during his explorations into realism in the Netherlands. For instance, *Memories of Dongxi* (《东溪回忆》) (2004.001) vividly captures a simple Chinese village market scene. A middle-aged farmer leads a donkey burdened with bundles, and the

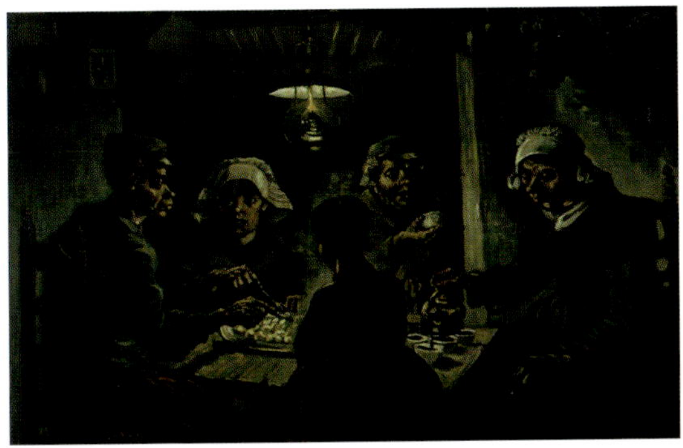

The Potato Eaters
Vincent van Gogh, 1885, Oil on canvas, 82 x 114 cm
Van Gogh Museum, Amsterdam, Netherlands

market-goers' weathered expressions complement their rugged attire. The village paths, uneven and mottled, are rendered by Xie Shan with strokes that appear straightforward, evoking the harsh realities of rural life. In terms of atmosphere, this series bears a resemblance to van Gogh's *The Potato Eaters*. While van Gogh infused a communal meal with a sense of religious ritual, Xie Shan's portrayal more directly reflects the arduousness of rural commerce and trade. In *The Potato Eaters*, van Gogh focuses on the workers' hands and a humble oil lamp, reinterpreting Leonardo da Vinci's *The Last Supper* with a stark tone to convey a sense of religious empathy. Xie Shan's *Memories of Dongxi* (《东溪回忆》) captures the painter's deep empathy with the labouring masses; his *Self-Portrait* (《自画像》) (2003.001) shares expressions with the characters in *Memories of Dongxi* (《东溪回忆》), both depicting the physical and emotional exhaustion endured under life's heavy burdens and, yet, demonstrating a determination to keep going. To evoke this sentiment, Xie Shan employs ochre and earthy yellows as primary colours, using blocks of rough texture to express a palpable heaviness. In his depictions of people, Xie Shan almost exclusively uses close-ups, distinguishing the portraits from their backgrounds through the use of colour blocks and temperature contrasts. His subjects' gazes do not meet the viewer's, suggesting a passive demeanour. Though Xie Shan's use of texture is coarse, he finely applies stippling techniques to create fluid highlights that vividly bring out the lifelike folds of both people and objects. Overall, Xie Shan's painting, and the world it reflects, seem to convey a life that, though tormented, refuses to succumb or retaliate violently. Instead, it embodies a passive yet resilient interpretation of existence – a distinctly Chinese approach to living.[8] Through Xie Shan's brush, life silently but persistently resists its fate. This 'storm-tested grass' resilience – relentless and unwavering – permeates Xie Shan's entire oeuvre.

Later in his career, much like van Gogh during his transition to impressionism in France, Xie Shan's palette brightened. Yet, his lines and overall layout retained a steadfast, quietly aspiring quality, steering clear of sweetness. Take, for instance, *A Place in Dongxi* (《东溪下场口》) (2019.001). In this work, Xie Shan's portrayal of trees leans towards Fauvist colour intensities, a significant shift from the spatial layering of hues in his earlier *Forest No.3* (《树林-3》). He preserves the luminosity through the textural contrasts between thin and thick applications of paint. Moreover, he masterfully conceals his own image within the field of colour. In the lower left corner, he seems to be wearing a red headscarf, with his gaze indiscernible, standing next to the trees. This technique of subtly incorporating his self-portrait into the canvas echoes practices employed by traditional Chinese painters and European Renaissance artists. Through this approach, the artist not only expresses his personal creative vision but also preserves his humility as a depictor; he remains reverent towards the scenes and characters and the very act of painting. This contrasts sharply with Dürer-style self-portraiture, which approaches a Christ-like depiction in its narcissistic portrayal. Indeed, showiness in art can often signify an artist's insecurity. Ancient Chinese artists are celebrated for having achieved a state of creative transcendence, whereby they became completely absorbed in their work. The allegorical stories of 'Disrobing and Becoming Unrestrained' (解衣磅

8. Joshua Gong, 2023, *Chinese Art Today: From 20th-Century Tradition to Contemporary Practice*, Lewes: Unicorn Publishing Group, p. 154.

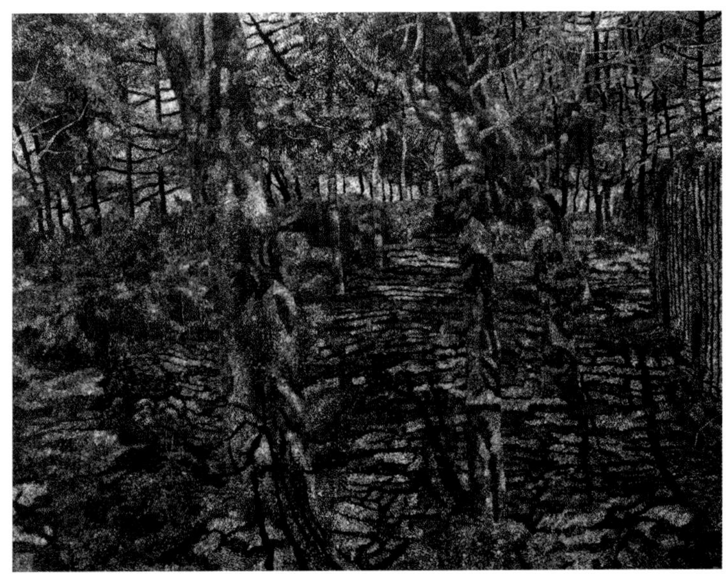

A Place in Dongxi 东溪下场口
2019, Oil on canvas, 30 x 24 cm

礴) and 'Butcher Ding's Skilful Dissection' (庖丁解牛) suggest that effortless mastery in art is a sign of having reached a mature level of both technique and philosophical understanding. *Warrior Entering the Palace* (《进入宫殿的武士》) uses a layout that intersperses the painter's perspective with life forms, showcasing Xie Shan's mature handling of the overall composition; in a complex yet balanced scene, it authentically reflects the painter's true state. Xie Shan's artworks are complex yet orderly, vibrant without being garish, and solemn without heaviness. Meticulous control and restraint in painting are profoundly linked to Xie Shan's journey to becoming a painter – a connection too significant to ignore. He exhibits tremendous confidence and dedication to his craft, having earned widespread admiration from

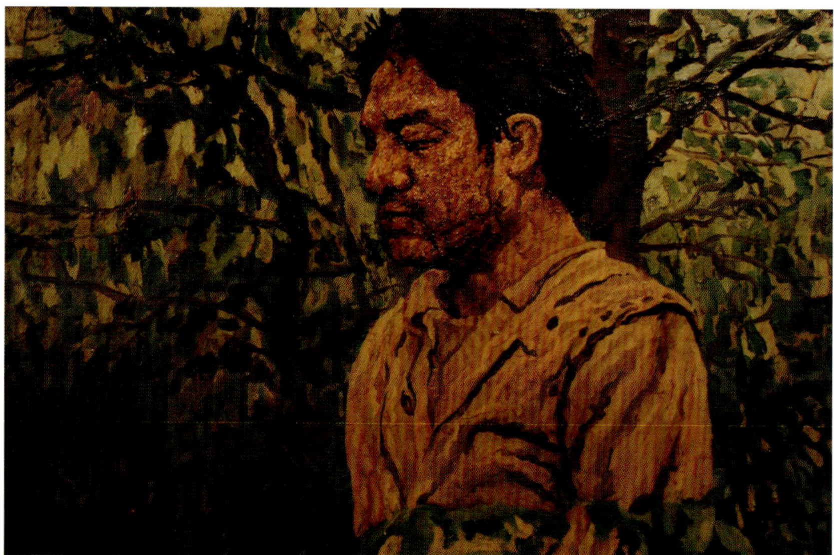

Self-Portrait 自画像
2003, Oil on canvas, 40 x 60 cm

peers across numerous exhibitions. Conversely, he shies away from sharing too much of his personal narrative, preferring instead to let his art act as a conduit for more organic forms of dialogue with his audience.

When painting portraits, Xie Shan focuses intensely on the eyes. The expressions captured not only convey the inner lives of the subjects but also reflect his distinctive observational technique. Afflicted with a conical cornea, Xie Shan's right eye once perceived the world in a way unlike others, leading to a vision so blurred it caused him considerable anguish. After a successful corneal transplant, he was restricted to painting just two hours per day, with the remainder dedicated to rest. Xie Shan values these two precious hours immensely, treating each painting session with meticulous attention. In his notably realistic *Self-Portrait* (《自画像》2003.001), Xie Shan is seen

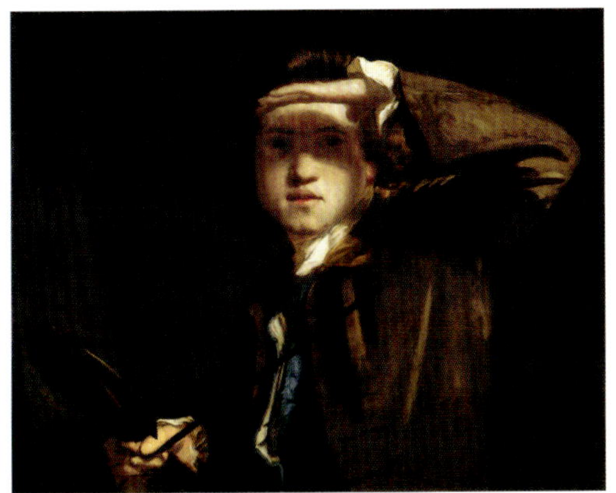

Self-Portrait
Joshua Reynolds, c. 1747–9
Oil on canvas, 63.5 x 74.3 cm
National Portrait Gallery, London, UK

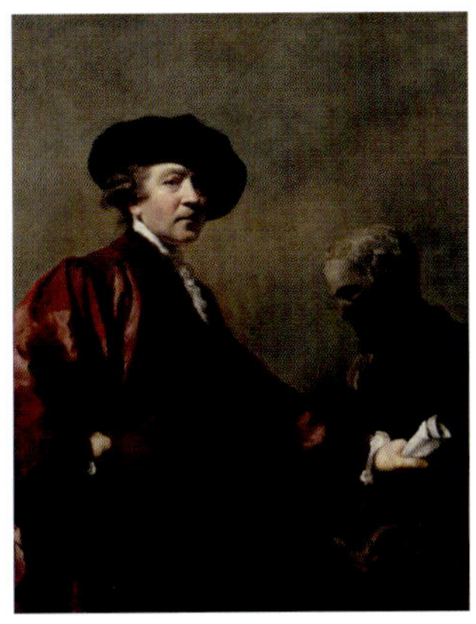

Self-Portrait of Sir Joshua Reynolds, PRA
Joshua Reynolds, c. 1780
Oil on panel, 127 x 101.6 cm
Royal Academy of Arts, London, UK
Photo credit: ©Royal Academy of Arts, London; photographer: John Hammond

in a forest, eyes closed, seemingly listening to the whispers of nature and sensing the interplay between his inner self and the external environment. The lively brushwork and tranquil expressions create a harmonious interplay. Xie Shan's self-portraits stand apart from those of his contemporaries. He depicts his painterly identity without the customary reliance on symbols such as painting tools or ornamental attire. Traditionally, self-portraits by painters feature elements such as brushes, palettes and smocks to affirm their professional roles. For example, Joshua Reynolds, the inaugural principal of the Royal Academy of Arts in the UK, produced an exemplary self-portrait in his youth (1747–9). In addition to using props, Reynolds's action of shading his eyes with his hand enhances the portrayal of a painter's acute awareness of light and vision. In another self-portrait painted around 1780, Reynolds styles himself as a classicist; he is adorned in a regal red

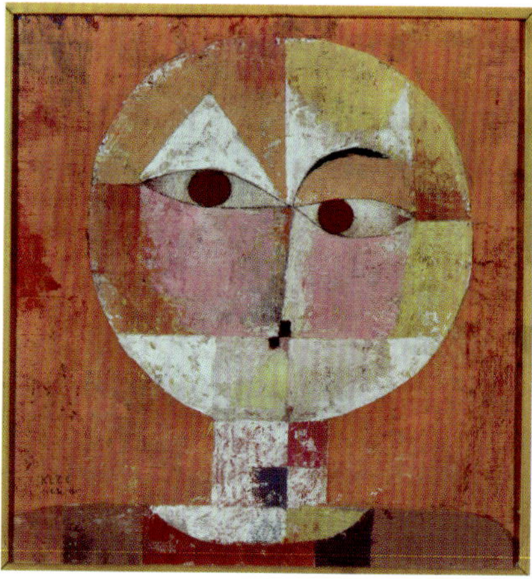

Senecio
Paul Klee, 1992, Oil on cardboard, 40.5 x 38.4 cm
Kunstmuseum, Basel, Switzerland
Photo Scala, Florence

robe and surrounded by classical Roman sculptures, thus distinguishing his intellectual stature from that of a mere craftsman. In Henri Rousseau's 1890 self-portrait, the painter appears in a black smock by a riverside, and an urban backdrop accentuates his identity as a painter within a capitalist society.[9] Xie Shan's self-portrait, much like many of van Gogh's, reveals his distinct painterly language without an over-reliance on additional illustrative elements. His works *Warrior Entering the Palace* (《进入宫殿的武士》) and *Warrior by the River* (《河边的武士》) can be interpreted as self-portraits. In them, Xie Shan allows himself to highlight the significance of his eyes through less-realistic representations. In these paintings, the eyes serve as both a key visual element and a tool, directly engaging the viewer while intentionally abstracting certain features of the characters through non-dimensional

9. Cornelia Stabenow, 2005, *Rousseau*, Cologne: Taschen, p. 19.

perspectives. By naming the self-portrait *Warrior*, Xie Shan communicates a societal aspect of his identity: he is continually engaged in a battle with destiny, and he is steadfast in his commitment to his art. This interplay in his artwork between object and self reflects a dynamic and evolving social interaction. Paul Klee's *New Face* (*Senecio*) is celebrated among modernist masters for initiating a shift in portrait painting that extends beyond the individual and explores the relationship between the portrait subject and the external world.[10] The intricacy, completeness and visionary approach of Xie Shan's *Warrior* series affirm his status as a modernist master. While he may not fully recognise it himself, his paintings distinctly manifest an avant-garde inclination.

The Painter's Self-Development:

Xie Shan eschewed conventional artistic training, instead forging his own distinctive painting style through self-directed study and life sketching. While self-taught artists are uncommon in history, they are indeed present. Among modernist artists, Henry Rousseau (1844–1910) and Francis Bacon (1909–1992) stand out as self-taught figures. Both were celebrated for their unique artistic voices, and they have been hailed as paradigms in global art history. Rousseau was based in Paris, the epicentre of artistic innovation during his time. He witnessed the birth and evolution of Modernism from the late nineteenth to the early twentieth century. Rousseau was part of a vibrant community that included luminaries such as Pablo Picasso, Guillaume Apollinaire, and Robert Delaunay, who were at the forefront of the artistic avant garde.[11] Their support and enthusiasm enabled Rousseau to adopt 'naive art' as his hallmark, carving out a niche within the avant-garde art community. Looser exhibition opportunities at venues such as the Salon des Refusés, the Autumn Salon and the Independent Salon in

10. Richard Brilliant, 1991, *Portraiture*, London: Reaktion Books, p. 67.
11. Cornelia Stabenow, 2005, *Rousseau*, Cologne: Taschen, p. 19–22.

Paris provided Rousseau and artists like him with a stage to freely express their unconventional talents.[12] Bacon, too, was a self-taught artist with a distinctively independent approach. He went even further than Rousseau, who was a symbol of the modern avant garde; Bacon's existentialist paintings heralded a new era. Early in his career, Bacon was considered an outsider artist (*sui generi*); yet his significant societal impact was recognised by the keen eyes of London's artistic elite. In 1929, Bacon established his studio in London. Not long after, he and a friend organised a joint exhibition. By 1933, his artwork was included in the influential book *Art Now* by the esteemed art historian Herbert Read, paving the way for Bacon's solo exhibition the following year.[13] Rousseau and Bacon both reaped the benefits of living in the cultural capitals of their times.

Raised in China during its Reform and Opening-up period, Xie Shan, likewise, found opportunities. He was nurtured in a warm, middle-class home. Today, China's decent social security and healthcare systems offer essential support to individuals like Xie Shan who face specific challenges. Still, Dongxi Town in Chongqing, unlike Paris as the nineteenth century turned into the twentieth, or interwar London, is far from being a center of global art. This context underscores the hurdles Xie Shan faced in his journey to becoming a painter, much more significant than any facing Rousseau and Bacon. With two decades of the twenty-first century behind us and postmodernism well integrated into China's cultural sphere, Xie Shan's artistic merits can be explored from various perspectives. In this age of globalism, Xie Shan's story and his art remain poignant testaments to a unique form of humanistic commitment and resolve.

After his fifteenth birthday, Xie Shan left formal schooling to fully immerse himself in painting and artistic creation at home. The early 1980s in China was a time when the restrictive Soviet-style artistic frameworks were being dismantled and the Chinese Artists Association was promoting a policy of artistic diversity. Initiatives from organisations such as the Sichuan Fine Arts Institute championed a resurgence of indigenous painting styles, heralding

---

12. Ibid.

13. John Russell, 1979, *Francis Bacon*, London: Thames and Hudson, pp. 16–20.

a new era in Chinese art. At this juncture, China was also opening its doors to globalisation. It began engaging more confidently in global collaborations and exploring art that resonated with both national and universal themes. The reinstatement in 1978 of the college entrance exam, after a decade without it, marked a significant shift; art institutions such as the Sichuan Fine Arts Institute began enrolling students normally again, including mature candidates, thus nurturing a generation of artists who ventured beyond traditional socialist realism.

While Xie Shan was developing his craft in solitude, the Sichuan Fine Arts Institute was evolving through various artistic phases including Scar Art, native realism, aestheticism, and expressionism. The vitality of the Sichuan Fine Arts Institute mirrored the broader transformation within the Chinese art scene. Artistry ran deep in Xie Shan's family: his mother was passionate about folk dance, his brother was a pianist, and his sister a singer—all possessed enduring commitment and determination to their artistic practices and ongoing training. Xie Shan inherited a remarkable trait of perseverance; he painted daily for decades, not wavering in the face of any setbacks or difficulties. His art evolved alongside his personal experiences, resulting in a diverse range of styles evident throughout his body of work. In the early 1980s, a variety of artistic styles – ranging from Western to Eastern and traditional to modern – began to be featured in art schools and publications. Fortuitously, Xie Shan had access to an extensive collection of art books from the outset, providing a rich repository of material for his study and exploration. As demonstrated by Francis Bacon, learning from printed materials does not compromise an artist's ability to create. Like Bacon, Xie Shan excelled at drawing inspiration from the masters featured in those books. He developed a painting language that was authentic to his own style, original in expression, and sincere in execution. As he was predominantly influenced initially by Western art, and because he mainly employed media such as sketching, watercolours and oils, traditional Chinese ink techniques appear less frequently in his works. Nonetheless, this does not imply that his paintings are devoid of Chinese elements. Xie Shan's original works are deeply rooted in his direct observations and interpretations of the environment and people around him. His creative source is the direct experiences and observations from contemporary Chinese society. His painting style does not begin with narrative themes like Western classicism, nor does it seek to express an ethereal essence as in traditional Chinese art; instead, he centres his art on the act and subject of painting itself. His artistic contemplation revolves around the cohesive integration of composition, form, colour and brushstrokes.

Xie Shan primarily explores themes such as idyllic memories of his hometown, critical reflections on war and urban fantasies. His early works demonstrated an analytical mindset reminiscent of Cézanne aimed at reordering painting, and he developed his own system: creating depth and richness on a flat plane through intricate detailing. His early paintings were marked by a delicate, luminous quality, but over time, he focused more on achieving a balance between colour and brushstroke, lending his later works a more mature and composed appearance.

At first glance, Xie Shan's use of light and shadow suggests a whisper of Impressionism; his landscapes recall the Russian Peredvizhniki movement; his scenic compositions mirror Cézanne's constructions; and his figures share a connection with Expressionism. Yet, any attempt to neatly categorise his work under established art historical movements seems inadequate. This uniqueness in his painting language underscores the originality of Xie Shan's art.

The standards for assessing a painter's value evolve with the times and with cultural shifts. Xie Shan's worth lies in his ability to develop a distinctive system within his painting language, driven by sincerity and persistence. Martin Kemp, an expert on Renaissance art, has pointed out that during the humanistic awakening, artists were particularly esteemed for three attributes: ingenuity (*ingegno*), creativity (*invenzione*) and imagination (*imaginativa*), qualities that complemented each other.[14] In contrast, ancient Chinese scholars appraised painters based on their unique artistic philosophies; the cultivated demeanour of the literati; and their enduring influence on

14. Martin Kemp, 1997, *Behind the Picture: Art and Evidence in the Italian Renaissance*, New Haven and London: Yale University Press, pp. 229–239.

subsequent generations. Gu Kaizhi, a proponent and practitioner of the 'spirit resonance' theory, is considered to be the first artist to have embodied these three esteemed qualities. In contemporary settings, the standards for assessing an artist's value are bound to shift with the changing times. Initially, the traditional scholar-gentry class of ancient China has receded, and the cultural ethos of feigning aloofness from art transactions is no longer predominant. Historically, literati paintings were commissioned through extensive, indirect communication, emphasising a subdued approach to artistic creation. The intricate relationships between patrons and creators significantly shaped the trajectories of artistic endeavours.[15] Furthermore, the age-old method of familial or master–apprentice training in China has increasingly been supplanted by formal education in public art schools. While art school training can lend a certain credence to emerging painters, the dynamic and versatile art market illustrates that such formal training is not indispensable for painters. Moreover, since the 1990s, the burgeoning Chinese art market has served as a litmus test of an artist's value, though market speculation and inflated prices have somewhat eroded the credibility of contemporary academic standards. Against this backdrop, Kemp's three qualities continue to be robust criteria for evaluating artistic merit. Xie Shan's work exemplifies these attributes, displaying a harmonious blend of genius, creativity, and imaginative prowess.

---

15. James Cahill, 1994, *The Painter's Practice: How Artists Lived and Worked in Traditional China*, New York: Columbia University Press, pp. 2–31.

Chapter Two: A Challenging Journey

"Someone has a great fire in his soul and nobody ever comes to warm themselves at it, and passers-by see nothing but a little smoke at the top of the chimney and then go on their way."

— Letter from Vincent van Gogh to Theo van Gogh[16]

Confidence and Healing:

The opening chapter of a biography often contains an obligatory treatment of the subject's family background. The emergence of a painter is deeply intertwined with their family environment and educational background. Painters seem to possess an inherent artistic sensitivity that distinguishes them from the beginning. After a painter achieves fame, those

16. 'Letter from Vincent van Gogh to Theo van Gogh,' *c.* 22–24 June 1880, Letter No. 155. <https://www.vangoghmuseum.nl/en/highlights/letters/155> (accessed 9 March 2024).

early signs are typically dramatised and portrayed as the seeds of their eventual success. Life – and, particularly, an artistic career – is rarely as neat as it is summarised in biographical accounts. Art historical texts, typically influenced as they by various motives, demand a discerning approach from their readers. This book strives not to unfold as a dense epic or a mere listing of facts, but, rather, to chart the authentic path of someone becoming a painter. What resonates most about Xie Shan's life and art is his sincere dedication to realising his ideals. Such sincerity is increasingly valuable in an age dominated by artificial intelligence. Xie Shan's story may reveal that becoming a painter is not solely a privilege reserved for the naturally gifted. Authentic thoughts and actions lend profound meaning to his story.

Xie Shan was born in 1968 and was fortunate to have grown up in a modest yet contented family. His parents were both educators – they were knowledgeable, rational and composed. His father was the principal of a middle school in Dongxi, Chongqing, and his mother taught at a kindergarten. Xie Shan, the youngest child, had both an elder brother and an elder sister. Such a family environment offered Xie Shan a nurturing and liberating environment. His parents and elder sister gave him considerable encouragement and positive guidance throughout his childhood. During his elementary school years, Xie Shan developed an interest in painting. At that time, he might not have fully grasped his situation; he was not academically distinguished among his peers. This affected him in several ways. First, Xie Shan felt guilty. As intellectuals, his parents had hoped he would inherit their academic abilities, and his struggles in this area greatly affected his self-confidence. Thankfully, his parents were supportive and did not reproach him for his academic challenges. Secondly, during a tumultuous era, Xie Shan's parents, as intellectuals, faced a societal backlash which placed the stigma upon their children of being born into a 'problematic' family. Influenced by these judgements, the children seldom questioned the unfairness of these perceptions.

Many of Xie Shan's classmates considered him to come from a 'bad family' and hesitated to interact closely with him. This had a knock-on effect on Xie Shan, who began to subconsciously believe that academic excellence was not for him. Due to the prevailing political sentiments, because they were educators, his parents were not afforded the respect or treatment they deserved. As a result of these pressures, Xie Shan's academic performance was mediocre. Additionally, his lack of social skills made him an outcast among his peers, and he was often subjected to bullying.

During that turbulent era, Xie Shan's father, who had moved south with the Second Field Army of the People's Liberation Army's political university, was branded a 'rightist' in 1957 and sent to rural labour reform, thus becoming a target of public criticism. And Xie Shan, as the progeny of what was derogatorily termed a 'stinky old ninth', faced exclusion by his peers, who blindly followed the prevailing sentiment. This likely contributed to his parents' persistent sense of indebtedness to their son. Later in life, Xie Shan's occasional outbursts of temper were always met with his father's unwavering tolerance. As an adult, Xie Shan often reflects with regret on his youthful misunderstanding of his father's actions.

The dilemma lies within the Confucian ethos that deems 'all pursuits inferior to scholarship'. In school, high-achieving students typically enjoy favoritism from teachers, parents and peers. Excelling academically, maintaining discipline, and being affable often positions a student as a role model, and parents will often point to such students as examples for their own children to follow. This is the principle behind the saying, 'To be near vermilion is to be stained red.' In contrast, students with average grades and introverted dispositions often find themselves marginalised in such an environment. Additionally, if a child exhibits poor behaviour, parents and teachers usually discourage other children from forming friendships with them, as per the adage, 'To be near ink is to be stained black.'

Xie Shan was a kind but academically unremarkable child. Consequently, he often battled feelings of inferiority, and he sought to validate his worth through a recognised skill. In the absence of frequent social interactions, painting became his refuge, a fitting solitary pursuit that allowed Xie Shan to retreat into a world uniquely his own.

When Xie Shan dedicated all his attention to painting and produced an exquisite piece, his classmates were immediately captivated by his artistic prowess. It turned out that Xie Shan was a painting prodigy! After receiving accolades from his peers, Xie Shan recognised that he could prove his worth through his distinct talents. This realisation spurred him to invest even more effort into his art. Upon discovering Xie Shan's passion for painting, his family was overjoyed. They offered him their unwavering support.

For young Xie Shan, painting was more than just a pastime; it was a transformative activity. First, painting allowed Xie Shan to retreat into a peaceful, personal sanctuary away from any turmoil. Secondly, his ability to focus on and excel in painting quickly attracted attention and positive reinforcement from classmates and family, thus bolstering his confidence in his artistic abilities. Thirdly, his interest in painting complemented his other hobbies. Xie Shan had a fascination with colourful military books and was well versed in Soviet military equipment. Camouflage patterns featuring in military magazines profoundly influenced the colour choices he employed in his artwork and enriched his artistic expression. The colours and designs of camouflage held a special meaning for Xie Shan. The camouflage patterns, familiar from childhood, not only acted as his best disguise but were also intricately linked to his unique visual experiences. Painting provided sanctuary for this sensitive and introverted painter, offering him a shield from the world and nurturing his self-care.

After completing junior high school, Xie Shan, with the support of his family, dedicated himself to painting at home. In the tranquility of his home, under the attentive care of his parents and elder brother and sister, he was able to immerse himself in art without external interruptions. When engaged in his art, Xie Shan could spend entire weeks indoors, focusing on completing a single painting. This intense focus surprised even him. Painting allowed him to lose himself, alleviating any feelings of loneliness and pain. He maintained this rigorous practice for several years.

At the age of twenty, he suddenly noticed his vision blurring during his painting sessions. His mother noticed that the objects Xie Shan painted began to distort into strange, twisted forms. As he painted portraits, the faces on his canvases grew increasingly indistinct, leaving him baffled about what was happening. Initially, Xie Shan had hoped that rest would remedy his vision, but after two years, there was still no improvement. His family took him to various hospitals and consulted numerous doctors across the city, yet they could not obtain a clear diagnosis.

After five months of uncertainty, a doctor, following multiple re-examinations, diagnosed keratoconus, a degenerative condition, in Xie Shan's right eye. This news was particularly distressing for him, as painting was his passion, and his deteriorating vision was severely impacting his ability to do it. At that time, specialists capable of treating keratoconus were scarce in Sichuan province, making the likelihood of restoring his vision slim. However, Xie Shan's family remained undeterred and finally located Dr Shen, a professor specialising in corneal transplants at Sichuan Huaxi Hospital. This doctor was exceptionally caring and professional, reassuring Xie Shan that the hospital would secure a suitable cornea for him and provide the highest standard of medical care. After a month in the hospital, Xie Shan was the recipient of a corneal transplant, the operation performed by Dr Shen. Five days post-surgery, when the bandages were removed from his right eye, Xie Shan was overjoyed to find he could see clearly once again; it was a massive relief after such a long ordeal.

Xie Shan now required glasses with a -5.00 dioptre correction, which improved his vision to 0.8, thus allowing him to continue painting without impediment. However, his body experienced some rejection effects relating to the new cornea. To alleviate the discomfort, he initially had to go to the hospital for injections each day for over a month, before switching to oral medication. From then on, Xie Shan could only paint for two hours before visual fatigue forced him to rest. Consequently, Xie Shan stopped doing outdoor sketching, instead observing and then mentally recreating scenes in his mind. He then painted these mental images during his two-hour daily painting sessions. During his rest periods, Xie Shan listened to symphonic music to adjust his state of mind. His favorite symphonies were by Tchaikovsky and Rachmaninoff (Сергей Васильевич Рахманинов). With the advent of smartphones, Xie Shan began using voice functions to listen to international news and updates on military equipment, a topic which had fascinated him since childhood.

In the early 1990s, Xie Shan started experiencing auditory hallucinations. While painting, he seemed to hear voices nearby, and they sounded to him as if somebody was harbouring ill intentions towards him. One day in September 1994, his condition worsened. He felt as if someone was chasing him, and he jumped out of a third-floor window to escape. Fortunately, Xie Shan's only injury was a broken right leg. This incident concerned his family deeply. In addition to having his right leg treated, they needed to get him help for his auditory hallucinations. Xie Shan was diagnosed with congenital schizophrenia and admitted to a psychiatric hospital for treatment.

After several years of treatment, Xie Shan's condition improved, allowing him to return home and resume painting. Following his father's death in September 1997, the family moved to Chengdu to live with his elder sister. Xie Shan's elder sister, who had better living conditions, consistently supported his artistic endeavours.

Upon leaving the hospital, he had begun to suffer from anxiety. The medication he relied on to stabilise his emotions caused hormonal imbalances in his body, and he put on thirty kilograms of weight. The medication also caused fluctuations in his hearing and visual sensitivity several days each week, hindering his ability to paint properly. When his brain was rested and he was ready to paint, his vision would often become fatigued. Thus, Xie Shan had to constantly find a balance between visual and mental fatigue. His already-limited daily two-hour painting sessions were further reduced to just a few hours over two or three days each week.

From 1999 to 2001, Xie Shan battled the constant side effects of medication. Sometimes, he couldn't even tell the time or discern his destination when riding a bus. The medication-induced anxiety flared up weekly. When he sensed the onset of anxiety, he would quickly return home, take his medication, and wait for it to take effect.

Despite these mental and physical limitations, Xie Shan did not despair. At least he could still paint. When he immersed himself fully in painting, he could forget all his pain and enter a world of freedom, relaxation and joy. In many ways, painting was his stabiliser – a balm for his ailments. To outsiders, Xie Shan's life appeared incredibly difficult. But for him, it was a daily reality. As long as he could paint, he did not feel overwhelmed by suffering. After 2002, Xie Shan's condition finally began to improve. The side effects persisted, but they became manageable.

Xie Shan initially lived at his sister's house, where she provided comprehensive care. Recognising that painting helped stabilise Xie Shan's condition, his sister offered her other residence for him to use as a studio. Although it was ten kilometres away, Xie Shan was overjoyed to have a dedicated space for his art. He walked to and from the studio every day. Within a year, he had overcome the obesity caused by his medication. Xie Shan's determination allowed him to persist in his chosen path and achieve remarkable results.

As time passed and Xie Shan aged, his mental state became more stable. He worked diligently, and his art matured accordingly. He began to look for a place where he could live independently. With his sister's help, he found a studio apartment on the top floor of a six-storey 1980s concrete block building, where he was able to live as independently as possible. He disliked noise, so his apartment on the top floor of a building with no lift was ideal for him.

In China, 1980s apartment buildings were better planned and had better plumbing compared to older urban houses; thus, living in the apartment was relatively comfortable. Despite this, as it was an old-style apartment, the sanitary conditions were challenging. Xie Shan's apartment was often visited by rats; sometimes, they would even gnaw on his canvases. But Xie Shan was unfazed. He completed one painting after another in that modest space. He lived there for over a decade. The landlord was moved by Xie Shan's dedication to his art and charged him an annual rent of only 10,000 renminbi. Although rents in China had doubled in that decade, his landlord never raised his rent.

Besides painting, Xie Shan had few material needs. He purchased high-quality art supplies, procuring the best pigments to enhance the visual impact of his paintings.

Learning and Vision:

Apart from painting in his studio and strolling in parks or in the countryside, Xie Shan rarely travelled. In 1998 he had begun attending the Sichuan Fine Arts Institute in Chongqing. However, his mental state at the time meant that he could not adapt to the pace and lifestyle there, so he had to return home to Chengdu. He eventually went back to Chongqing, but only to resume self-training.

In 2007, China's contemporary art market was flourishing, and there was a massive influx of foreign capital. Encouraged by this and supported by his sister, Xie Shan traveled to Beijing, particularly the 798 Art District, to experience the art scene and see if his work might find a discerning admirer. A cousin in Beijing helped arrange his travel. At that time, Xie Shan was in good health. With his cousin's help, he rented an affordable house in Huilongguan, within the Fifth Ring Road of Beijing. That year, Xie Shan spent most of his time painting at his residence and making frequent visits to the 798 Art District to immerse himself in the art scene. He introduced his paintings to gallery representatives and attracted considerable attention. However, when they learned he was self-taught, their interest waned. At that time in Beijing, artworks by graduates of prestigious institutions could sell for tens of thousands of renminbi. The market was so booming that many who had left the art field in the 1990s returned to seize the lucrative opportunities available.

Although Xie Shan didn't find a gallery or exhibition opportunity during his year in Beijing, he gained a lot. The 798 Art District was one of the most vibrant centres of contemporary art in the world. Many investors were anticipating the 2008 Beijing Olympics and the economic boom in China that was expected to accompany the Games. That year, many artworks were exhibited and exchanged in Beijing. This experience was eye-opening for Xie Shan, who had previously relied on printed materials to learn in the southwest of China. He had finally had the chance to engage closely with original artworks and the art market.

At that time, China's oil painting market had shifted from the idealised realism of Chen Yifei to abstract expressionism. Although new-media art, such as video installations, had been introduced to China in the 1980s and had been attempted by many artists, the overall market began accepting non-representational painting only around this period. The prices of Wu Guanzhong's near-abstract minimalist water town scenes soared. The purely abstract paintings of Zao Wou-Ki and Chu Teh-Chun also attracted significant attention and admiration. Xie Shan encountered numerous original works by Italian painters; their bold brushwork and vivid colours left a deep impression on him. This made Xie Shan realise that abstract expressionism might suit him better. Subsequently, Xie Shan's work transitioned from Georges Seurat's pointillism to Kandinsky's broad colour fields. He began experimenting with abandoning the palette and using primary colours and bold brushstrokes directly.

The US subprime mortgage crisis erupted in 2008, plunging the global economy into recession. China was one of the few economies to grow during this period, on the back of the Olympics and subsequent fiscal policies. These changes brought the Chinese art market into a period of transformation. The speculative money that had once flooded the market began to dissipate. Xie Shan concluded his year of study in Beijing and returned to his studio in Chengdu to begin a stylistic transformation.

In his new series, Xie Shan employed bolder brushstrokes, more direct colours, and whimsical geometric shapes. Although he didn't reap the financial benefits of the era in Beijing, the encouragement he received and the further development of his style brought him much solace. His paintings were filled with the joy of a successful transition.

In 2014, Xie Shan was invited by the Avant-Garde Contemporary Art Center in Nanjing to hold a solo exhibition. Titled *A Personal Arcadia*, his exhibition brought him recognition in the art world. Many media outlets and critics began to acknowledge the extraordinary emotional impact of Xie Shan's art and his inspiring story as a self-taught painter. In the contemporary art world, where the 'feast' had ended, it was rare for a painter without resources or background to gain such attention. One article commented on the Xie Shan phenomenon:

Although Xie Shan lacks formal training, he possesses the sensitivity and delicacy of an artist. The most touching aspect of his work is its sincerity. Over the years, contemporary art has focused on concepts, ideas, philosophy, or society. Yet, the primal essence of art and the sincere flow of human nature are slowly fading. This makes Xie Shan particularly precious.[17]

In 2023, Tong Gallery+Projects hosted a solo exhibition for Xie Shan in Beijing's 798 Art District. *The Knight of Wasteland* drew public attention once again. Critics noted that Xie Shan's art combined professional skill with the perseverance of a dedicated painter, and that its creation served as a form of self-healing for someone with mental illness.

A close look at Xie Shan's paintings reveals his consistent focus on history and European landscapes. This reflects a boy's rational approach to understanding a field – a characteristic trait for many adolescents. Mental illness gradually erodes the will of the sufferer, and in some cases this leads to more severe personality fragmentation in later years. Here, we see that, despite his illness, Xie Shan's mind and reason have remained intact. In his battle against schizophrenia, Xie Shan stands proud and resilient. He found art, and for him it was the best way to combat his illness. Moreover, Xie Shan's artistic achievements are not only significant to him alone. His works withstand professional scrutiny and are regarded as true art.[18]

From the recordings of some of Xie Shan's interviews, it is clear that he possesses a rational and highly articulate way of speaking. His 'mental illness' is merely a label that modern society assigns to a specific group. It suggests he is different, but it does not necessarily mean he has a disease. Everyone has emotions, and everyone experiences birth, ageing, sickness and death. These things are inevitable. His paintings are a blend of rationality and emotion. The uniqueness of his life journey has sparked his artistic genius. The path to becoming a painter was tortuous for him, but his works shine brightly.

---

17. '*Co-creating the Forest: Living by Painting for Half a Lifetime*', 19 June 2022, https://mp.weixin.qq.com/s/V5R6q19HUWRUI3JpG4U3lw (accessed 9 March 2024).

18. Zi Lin, *Shan Xie's Paintings*, 2023.

Chapter Three: A Symphony of Colourful Paintings

"Since I never attended art school, I have always painted according to my mood. I unconsciously discovered that when I feel depressed, I am less sensitive to colours. They blend together and lose their vibrancy, sometimes appearing dull. When I am happy, the colours are bright and joyful, with a natural beauty."

— Xie Shan

Xie Shan was born in the ancient town of Dongxi in Chongqing. This town is a historical and cultural site with over 1,300 years of history. It is located on the western bank of the Qijiang River, a tributary of the Yangtze River, between Chongqing and Zunyi. In ancient times, it belonged to the Ba State and came under the rule of the Central Plains dynasties from the Qin and Han periods onwards. Despite this history, Qijiang has not been a significant political, economic, cultural or military hub in China, nor has it produced many historically renowned figures. What it does offer is a leisurely tranquillity, a simple rural charm.

Xie Shan grew up in this picturesque place nestled between mountains and rivers, seemingly destined to live a peaceful life away from worldly strife. As the old saying goes, 'When Heaven is about to confer a great responsibility on a person, it first tests their resolve with hardship and adversity.' Xie Shan, from an ordinary town, faced many difficulties, which ultimately led him to choose the path of a painter.

Although Xie Shan was born in a relatively ordinary place, the greater Chongqing area and the Ba-Shu region hold places of significance in China's cultural history. The Ba-Shu region, also known as Sichuan, has historically been a crucial area for preserving Chinese civilisation due to its advantageous location between the Hengduan Mountains and the Yangtze River. Liu Bang, the founder of the Han Dynasty, launched a surprise attack on Hanzhong from Sichuan, overthrowing Xiang Yu and establishing China's first unified, centralised state. During the late Tang and Five Dynasties periods, Sichuan not only served as a refuge from war but it also nurtured a group of painters, a court flower-and-bird painting school represented by Huang Quan (903–965).

In modern times, Chongqing became the provisional capital of the Nationalist Government and was its stronghold during the War of Resistance against Japan. Many intellectuals from east and central China gathered in Chongqing, demonstrating resilience and fighting tirelessly for national independence and cultural preservation. The art world was no exception. Modern masters including Xu Beihong, Zhang Daqian, Lin Fengmian, Zao Wou-Ki and Wu Guanzhong converged on Chongqing, either creating art or engaging in art education, thus contributing significantly to the development of Sichuan's art scene. The Sichuan Fine Arts Institute in Chongqing became a crucial institution in the early stages of contemporary Chinese art, producing internationally renowned artists such as Luo Zhongli, He Duoling, and Zhang Xiaogang. While the ancient court flower-and-bird school may not have a direct connection to Xie Shan's era, the 'Sichuan Army Phenomenon' in contemporary Chinese art has had an influence on local artists. The example of world-renowned artist Zhang Xiaogang has particularly inspired many in the art community.

The above provides a brief introduction for readers, especially those unfamiliar with Chinese art, about the connection between Xie Shan's birthplace and Chinese art. Examining Xie Shan's artistic journey, readers can gain insight into aspects of contemporary Chinese art that diverge from traditional art. Xie Shan's work draws primarily from Western painting, closely linked to modern Chinese art education.

Traditional Chinese painting evolved through the awakening of the Wei and Jin dynasties and the multi-themed development of the Sui and Tang dynasties, and it reached its zenith during the Song and Yuan dynasties. Artists in the Ming and Qing dynasties focused more on preservation. Over a thousand years, paper and ink gradually replaced coloured murals as the medium of high art. A key difference in China's social development compared to that of the West and Japan was that during the Han dynasty, the aristocracy, which was based on lineage, was gradually replaced by a more culturally educated and mobile scholar-official class. By the Song dynasty, this class extended to lower levels of educated individuals. Consequently, Chinese art developed a strong inclination towards literati painting. The cultural discourse was dominated not by professional painters from the lower classes but by 'amateur' scholar-painters. Additionally, ancient Chinese society generally prioritised agriculture over commerce, leading to the development amongst painters of a moral imperative to 'value emotion over profit' (despite evidence having been found of literati painting transactions).[19] Consequently, in the later stages of traditional painting, art became a medium for literati revival or playful ink works, thus hindering innovation. This changed with the arrival of Western powers. The 'Four Wangs' painting system endorsed by the court and literati was challenged. Reform-minded scholars such as Kang Youwei, Cai Yuanpei and Chen Duxiu championed learning from the West, and they introduced the concept of

19. James Cahill, 1994, *The Painter's Practice: How Artists Lived and Worked in Traditional China*, New York: Columbia University Press.

'Chinese painting'.[20] The education system, originally centred on Confucian classics, was replaced in the late Qing dynasty by a system based on Western models. Painting, formerly an 'amateur' activity, was included in the new education curriculum.

The modern art system, referencing Western models, has continued in China to this day. Consequently, new forms of painting, for example, oil painting, gradually replaced ink painting and became mainstream in the art world. Painters Xu Beihong and Lin Fengmian were among the first to study in the Western art education system; they both chose to study in France and arrived there at around the same time. France, particularly Paris, was the centre of the art world at that time. Not only did France have the classical academic tradition from the Renaissance but it also led global trends with modernist movements.

The two masters, who had arrived in France at around the same time, brought back to China different Western art traditions. Xu Beihong believed that classicism was the key to reforming Chinese art. He thought the solid realism techniques of the French academic style were what Chinese literati painting most lacked. Lin Fengmian, on the other hand, embraced modernist painting, believing that vibrant and expressive styles were the foundation for integrating Eastern and Western art.

In his early years, Xie Shan primarily encountered art classics through Russian painting. The works that impressed him most were the landscape paintings of Ivan Shishkin (Иван Иванович Шишкин), a member of The Itinerants (Передви́жники). The Itinerants focused on everyday life and contemporary scenes, transforming the classical academic ideals of the French academy to reflect Russian life. Perhaps due to their fresh and natural visual appeal, the works of The Itinerants, especially the landscape paintings, held a strong attraction for Xie Shan.

As Xie Shan grew into his teenage years, China embarked on its Reform and Opening-Up, bringing more opportunities for painters to learn and grow. The change in outlook not only opened China to the world, introducing

20. Joshua Gong, 2023, *Chinese Art Today: From 20th-Century Tradition to Contemporary Practice*, Lewes: Unicorn Publishing Group, pp. 33–41.

advanced Western ideas and technologies, but it also revitalised national confidence and enthusiasm for modernisation and a better life, embracing principle of 'emancipating the mind and seeking truth from facts'. Influenced by the drive for sweeping change, young people eagerly pursued various fields of knowledge, including the humanities and arts. Western modernist and postmodernist art emerged simultaneously in China, challenging the academic tradition that had upheld historical narrative creation as the highest standard. This period saw the publication of new journals and art books and there were numerous exhibitions. Publications printed in colour became Xie Shan's best learning resources. Although there were few opportunities to see original classic art exhibitions in Dongxi, Xie Shan continued to study and improve his painting techniques by referring to printed materials.

In 1980s China, mechanical reproduction methods such as photography were not yet widespread. Consequently, the painters who had mastered Western realism were often regarded as having magical abilities. Xie Shan initially studied various Western realist artworks. He focused on techniques from the Renaissance, Dutch genre painting, the French academic style, and Russian realism to perfect his skills. Without access to original works, Xie Shan continually compared various reproductions and used sketching to reconstruct the visual language, aiming to approximate the originals. Many of his printed materials were in black and white only, and Xie Shan had to use light and shadow to infer the colours. Over time, he developed his own methods to compensate for the limitations of mechanical reproduction. This inadvertently trained him in the techniques he would later need in his creative work.

For instance, in copying Théodore Géricault's (1791–1824) *The Raft of the Medusa*, Xie Shan employs a black ink pen. He structures the composition through varying line densities and directions. Horizontal lines are used to depict the clouds; angled lines capture the turbulent waves; short lines convey the raft's texture; and a complex interplay of dashed and solid lines describe the movements of the figures on the raft. Although Xie Shan's piece is a reproduction, it showcases his natural talent for learning the language of painting and his remarkable determination and ability to

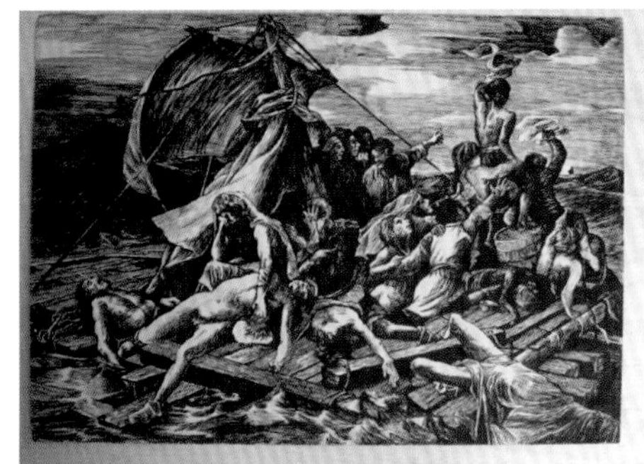

The Raft of the Medusa after Théodore Géricault
1983, Ink on paper

solve pictorial challenges with limited resources. Many admirers of modernist painting might recall Cézanne's famous dictum: 'We must treat nature through the cylinder, the sphere and the cone.'[21] Cézanne elaborated on this idea with a discussion about lines which shares similarities with Xie Shan's sketching techniques:

> *Lines parallel to the horizon give breadth... Lines perpendicular to this horizon give depth. But nature for us men is more depth than surface, whence the need to introduce into our light vibrations, represented by the reds and yellows, a sufficient amount of blueness to give the feel of air.*[22]

Cézanne's statement, through formal analysis from a painter's perspective, explains some of his painting methods. In the West, many believe Cézanne liberated painting from merely recording reality. After

---

21. Paul Cézanne, 1904, 'Letter to Emile Bernard', in *Art in Theory 1900-2000: An Anthology of Changing* Ideas, 2003, New Edition, eds Charles Harrison and Paul Wood, Oxford: Blackwell Publishing, p. 33.

22. Ibid.

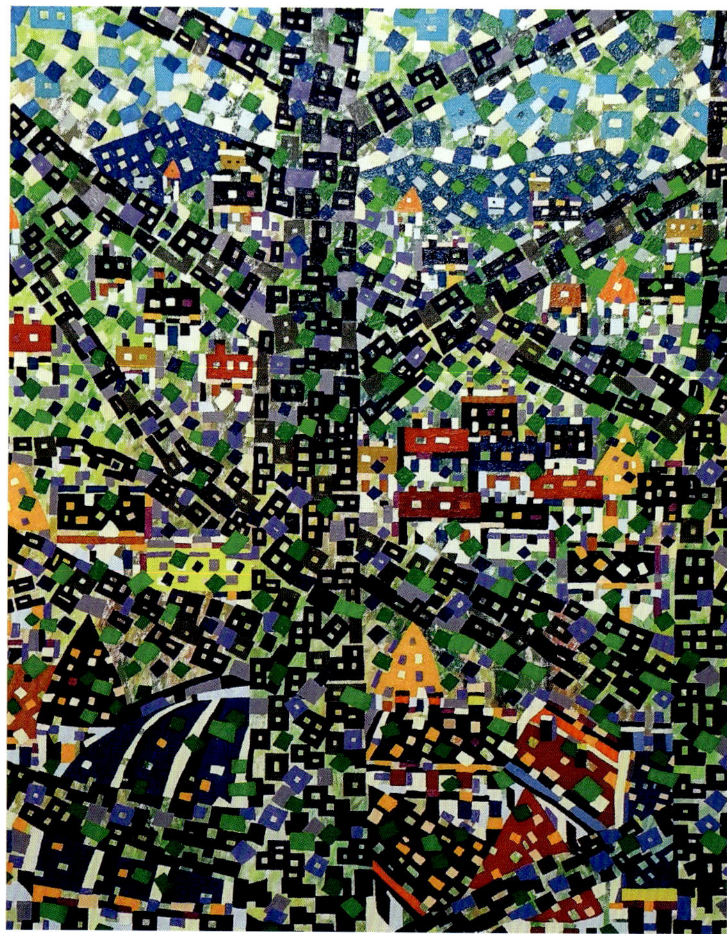

European Woods 欧洲树林
2019, Oil on canvas, 80 x 60 cm

Cézanne, painting, as an art form, achieved independence.[23] Xie Shan may not have read the Chinese translation of Cézanne's letters, but his still-life studies suggest he has researched Cézanne's techniques, internalised the concepts and developed his own unique style.

In a reproduction of a Dutch riverside cityscape, Xie Shan demonstrates new interpretations. He employs more orderly and gentle lines to simplify the composition. The horizontal lines of the sky and a few vertical strokes of buildings create a spatial contrast. Windows, railings, the riverbank and reflections in the water are rendered with increased negative space. This technique directs the viewer's focus to the central figure – a young girl with a headscarf, deep in thought by the riverside. This study contrasts vividly with the technique used in *The Raft of the Medusa*, demonstrating that Xie Shan, even while copying, can tailor his brushwork and rhythm to match the scene's atmosphere, finding a more suitable language to convey the painting's emotions in his reinterpretation.

Xie Shan's painting skills have progressed rapidly due to his versatile brushwork and experience in reinterpretation. Xie Shan began creating his original works by engaging with the works of Western masters.

The unwavering support of his family has been a strong foundation for Xie Shan's dedication to painting. His mother loves performing traditional dances and has maintained this passion for decades. His brother enjoys playing the piano and still practices for an hour every day. He moved to Budapest for work and settled in that classical music haven, fulfilling his childhood dream of living in a city of culture.

Xie Shan frequently learns about the European experience from his brother, enabling him to construct a vivid artistic world in his mind. Many of Xie Shan's paintings inspired by European reveries are deeply connected to his longing for his brother. In *European Woods* (《欧洲树林》) (2019.004), Xie Shan uses a flat perspective, overlaying aerial views of European roads and houses with landscapes, creating grids of squares and circles. In the grid, black blocks depict tree trunks and branches, interspersed with

23. Richard Verdi, 1992, *Cézanne*, London: Thames and Hudson, p. 15.

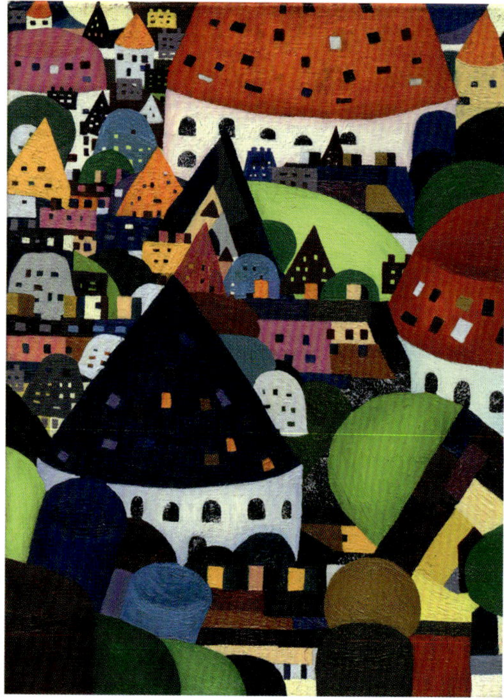

Memories European Impressions No. 4 回忆 欧洲印象 **4**
2020, Oil on canvas, 35 x 25 cm

monochromatic blocks. The yellow and green on the left side of the painting echo the multicoloured houses on the right. The blue in the lower-left corner suggests a winding river, while the black and ochre in the lower-right corner might represent a school running track or the grounds of an industrial park. The zigzag at the top of the painting forms a hillside of pale blue blocks, with sky blue squares overlapping green and white ones at the very top to form the sky. Although Xie Shan appears to use the surrealist paranoiac–

critical method in this painting, his planar composition retains a Cézanne-like control over the elements. The paranoiac–critical method, proposed by Salvador Dalí, is a painting technique that uses optical illusions to evoke a secondary visual symbol in the viewer's mind, thereby expanding the original image's meaning.[24] Conceptually, André Breton believed this invoked a fundamental crisis in the meaning of the object. These ideas emerged as surrealists sought new possibilities in painting. However, for Xie Shan, these conceptual interpretations or assumptions were not the foundation of his practice.

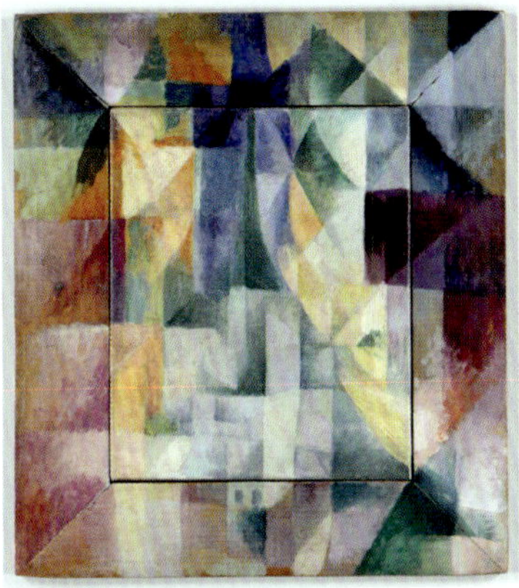

Fensterbild (Window Picture)
Robert Delaunay, 1912, Oil on canvas, 46 x 40 cm
Hamburger Kunsthalle, Germany
Photo Scala, Florence/bpk, Bildagentur für Kunst, Kultur und Geschichte, Berlin

At first glance, *European Woods* (《欧洲树林》) may appear somewhat Cubist or Surrealist. However, on closer examination, it is evident that Xie Shan's spatial constructions and painting language are closely intertwined with his personal state of mind. His technique is based on a self-developed logic. In certain respects, it resembles Western modernism, but in terms of painting habits and tendencies, these works are unmistakably postmodern. In the 1970s, Western art underwent significant changes. The exploration of artistic media, from Post-Impressionism to Conceptual Art, reached a standstill. The practice of Marcel Duchamp's (1887–1968) concept of visual service became increasingly difficult as the exploration of anti-material art deepened. Andy Warhol's (1928–1987) mechanical reproduction overturned the concepts of gesture-based action and absolute authority showcased by American Abstract Expressionism, both academically and in the market. Discussions

---

24. Robert Adèle Greeley, 2001, 'Dalí's Fascism; Lacan's Paranoia', *Art History*, Vol. 24, No. 4, Sept, pp. 465–92. <https://academic.oup.com/arthistory/article-abstract/24/4/465/7278632?redirectedFrom=fulltext&login=false>, (accessed 9 March 2024).

of postmodernism, the end of art, and the end of art history began to emerge in academic circles.[25] By the 1980s, some artists had begun to return to the essence of painting, redefining its possibilities through cross-media and anti-material explorations. German Neo-Expressionism used painting to express conceptual art ideas. Anselm Kiefer, in particular, depicted the weight of historical spirit on canvas, grounded in European historical realities.[26] Unlike German neo-expressionists like Kiefer, Xie Shan's portrayals of Europe are based on imaginative scenes from indirect sources rather than direct cultural contexts.

The psychoanalyst Janine Chasseguet-Smirgel (1928–2006), in her exploration of the 'ego ideal', noted that 'The human being "needs others to hold out a mirror so that he may contemplate what he sees there without feelings of self-hatred or self-adoration; deprived of this, he would die, or cease to progress."'[27]

Xie Shan's *European Impressions* (《欧洲印象》) series (e.g. *Memories European Impressions No.4*, 2020.003) distils the unique architecture of European cities into geometric shapes, beautifully complemented by harmonious colours. Unlike the Orphism praised by Guillaume Apollinaire, this imaginative painting is a thoughtful construction of the European images in his mind. Apollinaire admired Robert Delaunay's Paris cityscapes, such as *Fensterbild (Window Picture)*, for capturing the simultaneity characteristic of modernism:

> *Simultaneity is life itself, and in whatever order the elements of a work succeed each other, it leads to an ineluctable end, which is death; but the creator knows only eternity. Artists have for too long strained toward death by assembling the sterile elements of art, and it is time they attained them, not only in words, but also in his works – pure painting, reality.*[28]

---

25. Théo de Luca, 2020, *A New Spirit in Painting*, 1981: On Being an Antimodern, London: Koenig Books, p. 17; Arthur Danto, 1997, New Jersey: Princeton University Press, p. 33.

26. Donald Kuspit, 1993, *The New Subjectivism: Art in the 1980s*, New York: Da Capo Press, p. 18.

27. Ibid., p. xxii.

28 Guillaume Apollinaire, 1912, 'Reality, Pure Painting', in *Apollinaire on Art: Essays and Reviews* 1902-1918, 2001,

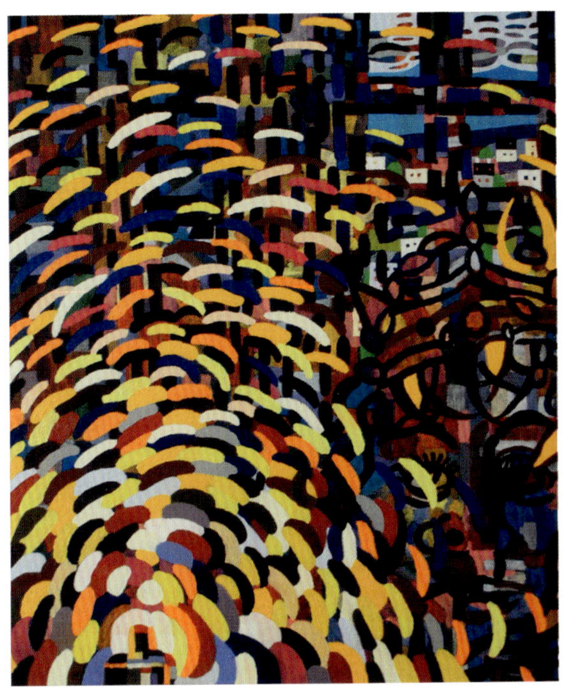

A Weaver 纺织姑娘
2020, Oil on canvas, 60 x 50 cm

The simultaneity in Xie Shan's *European Impressions* is not about simple contrasting colours and their resulting illusions. Instead, it reflects the mutual influences and imaginations of civilisations from a global perspective, leading to new combinations and extensions.

While also a cultural imagination, Xie Shan's works differ from some German neo-expressionist paintings by removing the weight of history and

---

ed. Leroy C. Breunig, transl. by Susan Suleiman, Boston: MFA Publishing, p. 256.

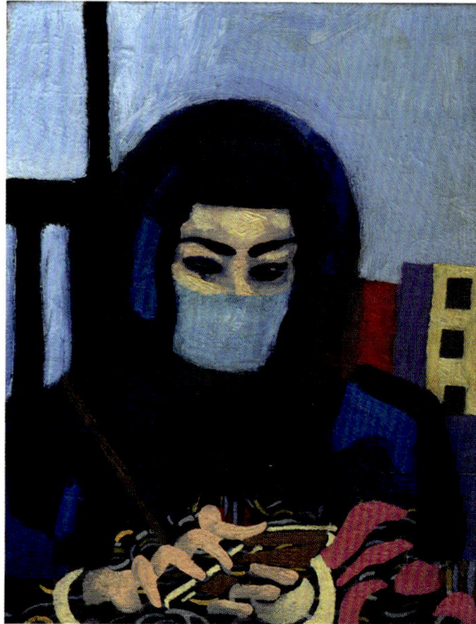

On the Bus 公交车上
2019, Oil on canvas, 40 x 30 cm

infusing universal elements of family, friendship and a sense of place. The historical burden of Chinese culture is profound. For a long time, following the ways of ancient kings was preferred over those of later rulers. Xie Shan was fortunate to live through the Reform and Opening-Up period, a time of rapid development that transformed society. In the past century, China has faced numerous upheavals and once again withstood the tests of history. Despite clashes, China's four-thousand-year-old culture has endured tenaciously.

Ancient Chinese poetry often celebrates simple personal emotions. For instance, classics like *Guan Ju* (《关雎》), *The Peasant* (《氓》) and *The Reeds and Rushes* (《蒹葭》) use plain language and universal feelings

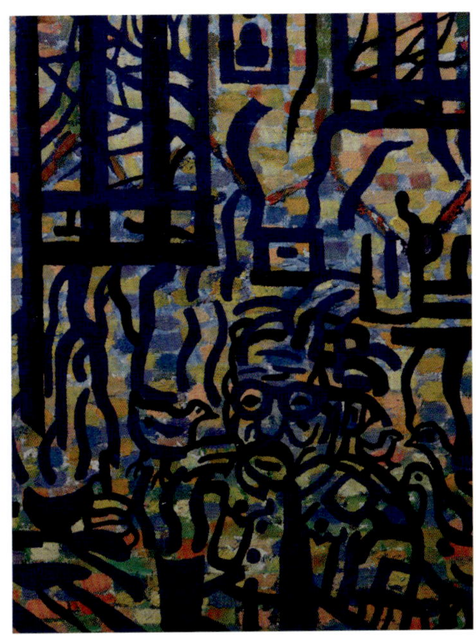

Downtrodden Father 落魄的父亲
2022, Oil on canvas, 47 x 37 cm

to convey poetic imagery. Similarly, Xie Shan's *A Weaver* (《纺织姑娘》) (2020.013) adopts a style reminiscent of Delaunay's *Windows* series, expressing his longing for the scenes outside the window – a distant and beautiful imagination. His brother's move to Budapest opened a window for Xie Shan, connecting him to modernist painting. His narrative paintings do not focus on retelling a single, linear story or a momentary emotion; instead, they reflect the painter's desire to depict through multiple perspectives and a divergent approach. As contemporary art historian Tony Godfrey pointed out, in their narratives, contemporary painters:

> *...give us an experience about narrative, or an experience like narrative, but with no linear progression. Whereas a nineteenth-century painter would have tried to illustrate a dream, now painters would rather make the painting function like dream-work. We have to find our own way.*[29]

An early painting by Xie Shan depicted his brother playing the piano while his sister stood listening. Although the painting captures a single moment, the dynamic hand movements and flowing clothes of his brother evoke a sense of movement and continuity.

This depiction of dynamic figures has been retained in Xie Shan's work since his stylistic adjustment in 2018. In *On the Bus* (《公交车上》) (2019.002), Xie Shan uses a minimalist approach with smooth brushstrokes to vividly portray a woman wearing a mask. A mobile phone rests between her slender fingers. In the predominantly blue-toned portrait, the woman's warmly toned fingers and pink accents enliven the composition. In *Downtrodden Father* (《落魄的父亲》) (2022.003), Xie Shan uses curves to depict the dynamic figure of the bespectacled father and straight lines with warm colours for the architecture and background. The image of the father blends into the flat background. Although the title suggests a downtrodden father, the presence of poultry around him reveals his loving nature. This painting reflects Xie Shan's longing for his father and his feelings of guilt. He recalls how his father was always very tolerant of his childhood whims, doing everything possible to help him overcome external disturbances and worries. Xie Shan's portraits, while showcasing his unique technique, are always imbued with warmth.

Whether painting landscapes, still lifes, figures or imaginary scenes, Xie Shan's gentleness and inner brightness shine through. Postmodern society offered Xie Shan acceptance, his warm and harmonious family provided him with warmth; and art gave him life. Xie Shan's art and story are a product of self-choice. His pure and bright inner world allows his art to maintain such honesty and warmth. He never hides his envy of peers who have families and

29 Tony Godfrey, 2020, *The Story of Contemporary Art*, London: Thames and Hudson, p. 185.

children, nor does he conceal his hope that his paintings will be loved by the public. Yet, he always concludes with gratitude: 'Painting made me a painter, and I am content and very happy.'

Sartre, when expounding on existentialism, wrote:

> *The other is essential to my existence, as well as to the knowledge I have of myself. Under these conditions, my intimate discovery of myself is at the same time a revelation of the other as a freedom that confronts my own and that cannot think or will without doing so for or against me. We are thus immediately thrust into a world that we may call 'intersubjectivity'. It is in this world that man decides what he is and what others are.*[30]

Xie Shan's paintings create an 'interactive subjective' world where viewers can reflect on their own kindness and innocence.

30 Jean-Paul Sartre, 2007, *Existentialism is a Humanism*, ed. John Kulka, transl. by Carol Macomber, London: Yale University Press, pp. 41–42.

Chapter Four: The Artist's Works and Self-Reflections

"How beauteous mankind is!
O brave new world, That has such people in't."

—Shakespeare, *The Tempest*

In recent years, Xie Shan's artistic achievements have been gradually recognised by the industry, bringing with it certain impacts from fame and fortune. After his successful solo exhibition *A Personal Arcadia* in Nanjing in 2014, he found himself at a creative crossroads. The positive feedback on his *Forest Series* at the exhibition made him feel that this was his most appreciated work. Consequently, Xie Shan's creative thinking and confidence became confined to this particular subject and style. This limitation was clearly detrimental to his artistic development.

Artistic value is constructed within a cultural context. Historically, the

Medici family promoted the Renaissance. In the early modernist period, American art dealers helped secure Impressionism a place in the European value system. Matisse was encouraged by the Russian merchant Sergei Shchukin, leading to the creation of his Fauvist *La Danse* series. Picasso gained the favour of Gertrude Stein, which elevated the prominence of his Cubism. Exceptional art patrons and promoters can help artists gain recognition and positive feedback and maintain a sincere attitude towards art despite misunderstanding or excessive praise. For Xie Shan, art manager Xiao Bin serves as such a patron.

Xiao Bin was keenly aware when Xie Shan experienced confusion about his artistic direction. He chose not to intervene directly, allowing Xie Shan to struggle and think and thus free himself from the illusions and burdens of 'success'. When capital sought to exploit art for quick profits, Xiao Bin stood between them and the artist, often cooling their enthusiasm, to protect Xie Shan's creative environment. Xiao Bin's interventions were directed at capital; he hoped Xie Shan would find his own way out of the bottleneck.

Xie Shan's perseverance and insight eventually led him out of his illusion. His newer works showed that he had surpassed his previous limitations in technique and subject matter, and he gained more recognition from industry professionals. Xie Shan embraced a brave new world[31], finding balance between chaos and order in his artistic realm. Freedom grows in the interplay between emotion and reason.

Xie Shan's self-reflections on his work convey a tangible and more direct sense of art, confidence and freedom.

On the European Fantasy series:

How do you capture the unique features of imagined European scenes?

I aim to convey a rich and varied landscape through these paintings.

31 The 'civilised society' imagined by British writer Aldous Huxley.

I use cool and warm tones, geometric shapes, and diverse elements to give the composition depth and rhythm. For example, I use finer brushstrokes to detail small elements, adding intricacy and rhythm to the entire piece. To better capture the European essence, I intentionally use warm colours like red and purple for the rooftops.

Why use a lot of geometric colour blocks?

It's primarily for composition and element consideration. Using geometric shapes allows me to highlight the characteristics of European architecture, making the composition more visually striking and impactful. Additionally, I hope to explore new painting styles and modes of expression through this method.

Why use colours full of fairy tale and fantasy?

I want to bring the audience a sense of joy and relaxation, so I chose bright and playful colours. Long periods of creating can make me feel fatigued and bored, so I try a different style to find new inspiration. European painting theories and styles have greatly inspired me. I hope to express my feelings by incorporating these elements. This new approach to creating is both a challenge and an innovation for me, and it brings me great joy.

Why is the use of blue tones particularly prominent in your work?

I choose blue tones because I find them more 'grounded.' Compared to the green tones I used frequently before, blue is more stable and has more depth. Additionally, the richness of blue tones provides me with vast creative possibilities. Lake blue, ultramarine, sky blue, deep blue, cobalt blue... these different shades of blue can all present unique nuances in my work.

Reflections on anti-war themes in the Ancient Battlefield series:

European ancient battlefields are rich in history and narrative, providing me with abundant creative inspiration. To authentically capture the era's atmosphere, I collected historical materials and books. The brutal ambience of the battlefield left a deep impression on me. However, I do not wish to overly depict the bloodiness of war. I prefer to present battlefields with a sense of childlike innocence and wonder. Many realistic battlefield paintings exist in history, so I wanted to explore a different expression, aiming for a more pleasant depiction. Although war itself is cruel, I hope to portray it in a more interesting and innocent manner. I experience a lot of pressure myself and do not want to pass this on to the audience. I hope my work can bring people a sense of joy and relaxation.

Is depicting battlefields contradictory to anti-war sentiments?

There is indeed a contradiction. But I believe that when depicting war, it's important to reflect the historical context and the reality of the battlefield. Therefore, I include elements like swords, shields, and armour to enhance the authenticity. However, I present these elements in my own way, blending historical accuracy with a touch of childlike innocence. My works do contain critical elements. I choose to paint ancient Chinese and European battlefields because they were bloody, and that's a fact. I hope to use my art to criticise the cruel aspects of human history. At the same time, I try to depict a sense of innocence and beauty on the battlefield to express my hope and ideals for the future. Living with ideals and hope drives people forward. I want my paintings to show a beautiful future. Additionally, I aim to deeply criticise the brutal aspects of human history through depicting ancient battlefields, awakening a pursuit of peace and beauty.

How does depicting ancient battlefields express criticism of contemporary society?

The issues reflected in ancient battlefields are enduring human problems that transcend time and space, possessing universal relevance. By depicting ancient battlefields, I can delve deeper into the cruel aspects of human history, prompting people to reflect on these issues. I believe contemporary society still has many injustices and inhumane practices. These problems need to be faced and solved collectively. As a painter, I express my views and feelings on these issues through my work, hoping to draw more attention and provoke thought. At the same time, I hope to convey a positive force through my work, encouraging people to strive for a better life and future. I believe contemporary society still has many injustices and inhumane practices. These problems need to be faced and solved collectively. As a painter, I express my views and feelings on these issues through my work, hoping to draw more attention and provoke thought. At the same time, I hope to convey a positive force through my work, encouraging people to strive for a better life and future.

On the Hometown Memories series:

I use bright colours and simple lines to recreate my ideal hometown. These colours and atmospheres reflect my fondest imaginings. Through painting, I find comfort, as if I've returned to that joyful and warm place.

I believe a good work must come from genuine life experiences. Whether it's memories of my hometown or moments from city life, these are things I've truly felt. I transform these feelings into paintings through recollection and reconstruction. I don't paint strictly from photos or objects. Instead, I incorporate my imagination and interpretation to make the images more vivid and interesting.

Memories are a beautiful thing; they allow us to relive the good times of the past. Through painting, I can turn these memories into tangible images, giving them permanence in my work. At the same time, I add my imagination and interpretation, making the images align with my ideal vision.

On cityscape paintings:

These paintings capture and reconstruct beautiful moments from my life. For instance, the painting of the little girl eating in a fast-food restaurant comes from my cherished memories of dining there many times. The environment was very quiet, and the little girl eating peacefully left a deep impression on me. So, I captured that beautiful moment through painting.

Artworks

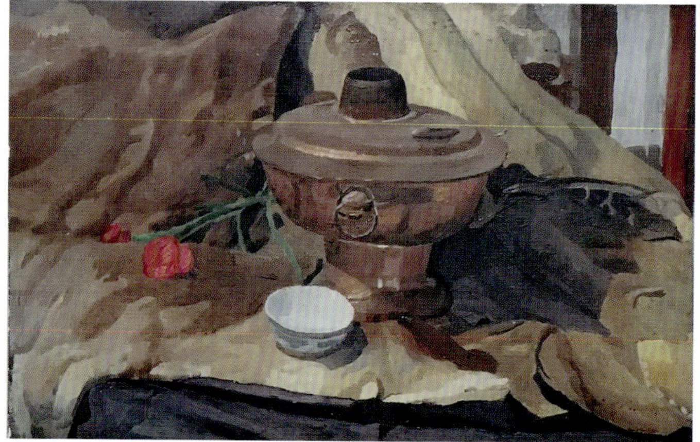

Copper Hot Pot
铜火锅
1998, Oil on canvas, 50 x 76 cm
1998.001

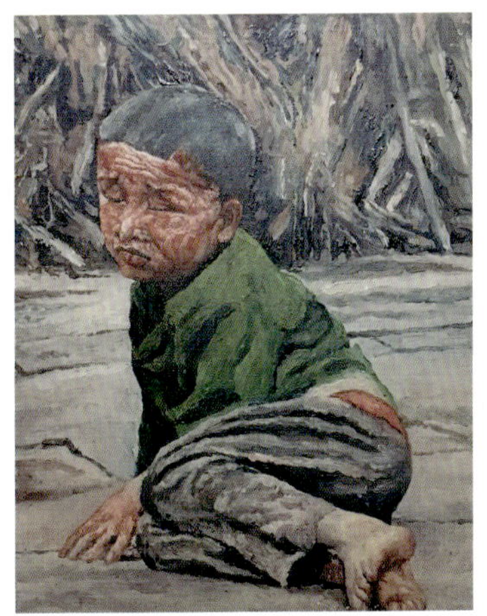

Memories of Dongxi
东溪回忆
1998, Oil on canvas, 80 x 60 cm
1998.002

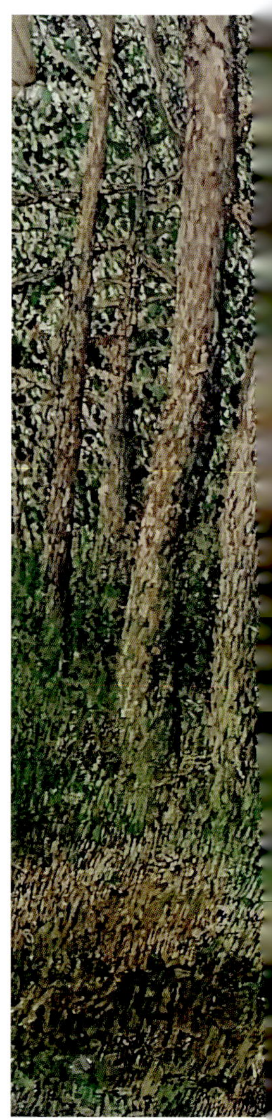

Back Hillside of Qijiang
綦江后山坡
2000, Oil on canvas, 78 x 62 cm
2000.001

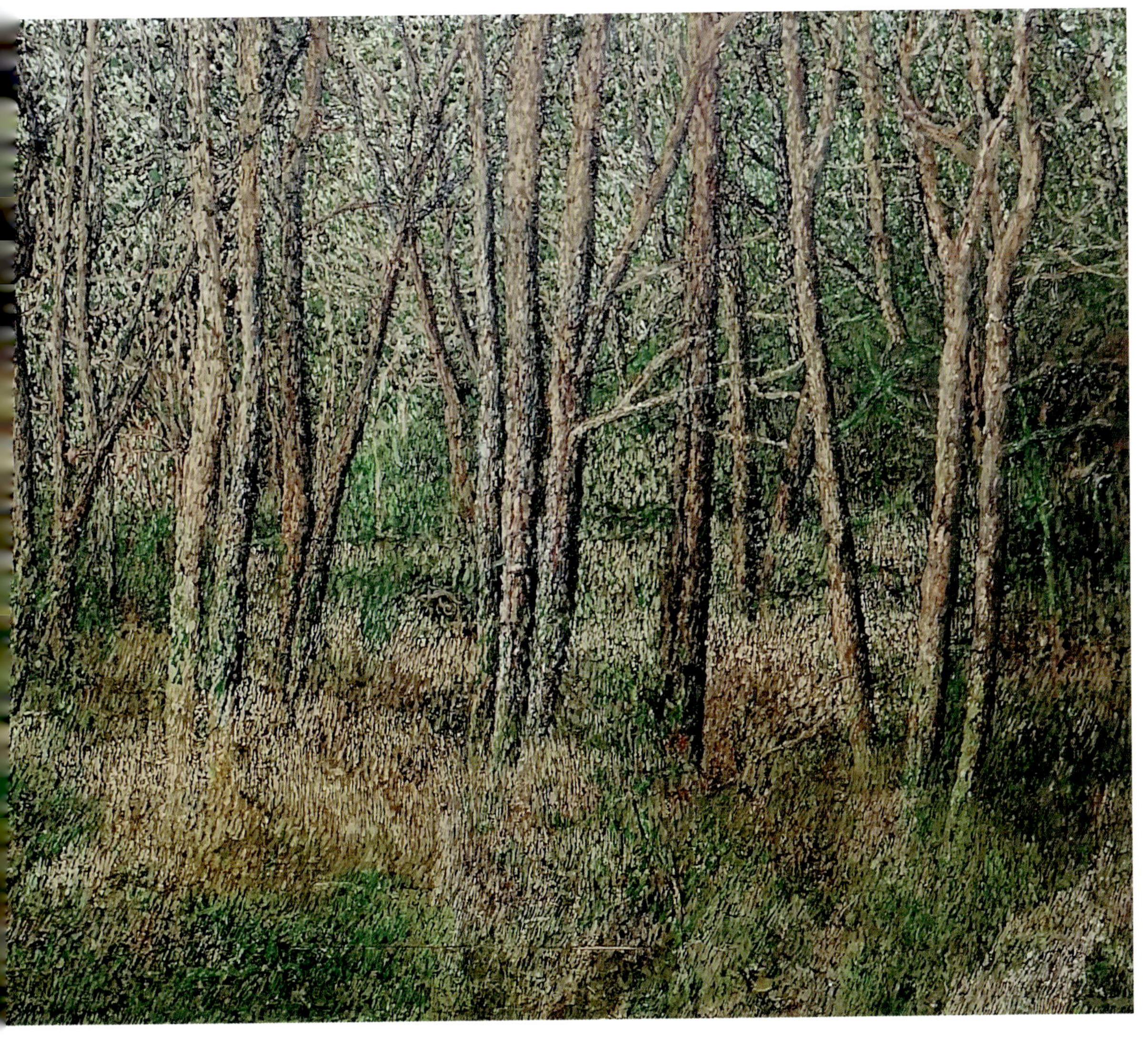

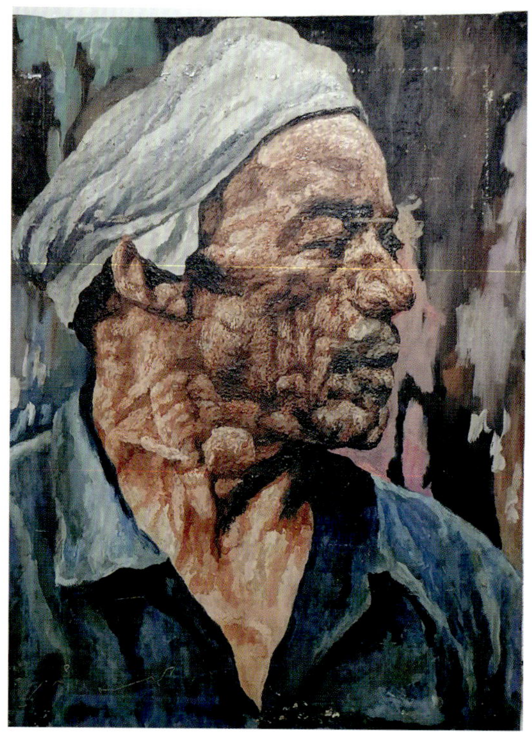

A Wedding in Dingshan Township, Dongxi
东溪丁山乡主持乡下婚礼的农民
2000, Oil on canvas, 88 x 63 cm
2000.002

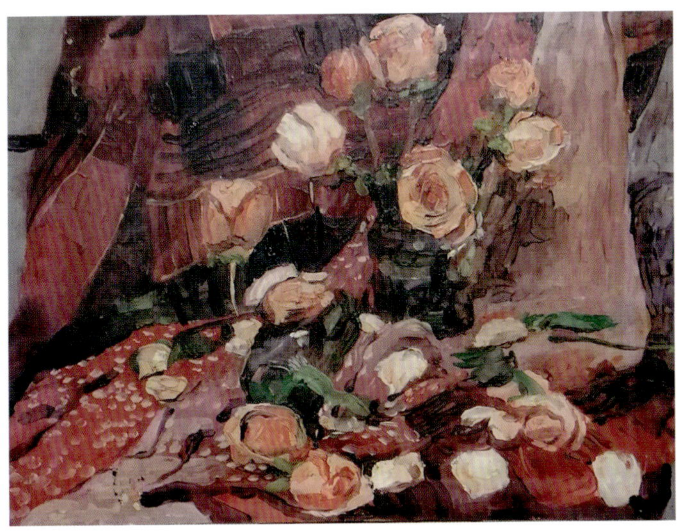

Flowers
鲜花
2001, Oil on canvas, 54 x 68 cm
2001.001

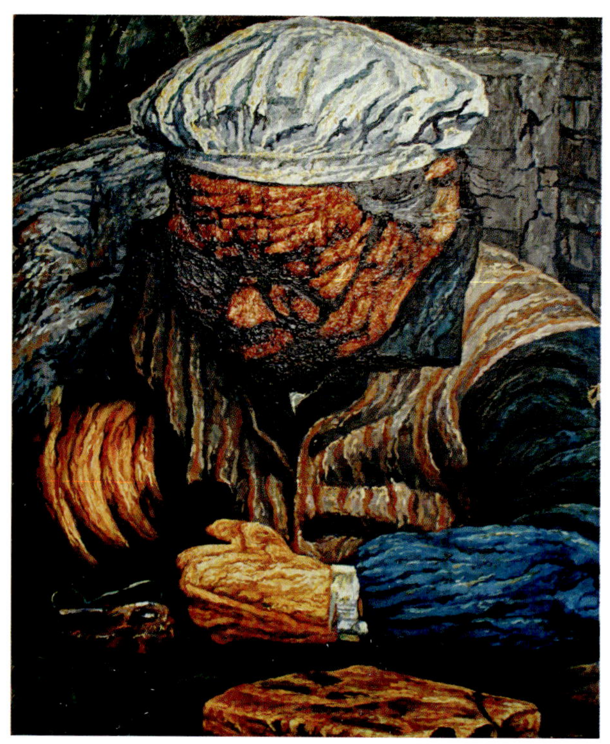

Memories of Dongxi
东溪回忆
2002, Oil on canvas, 60 x 80 cm
2002.001

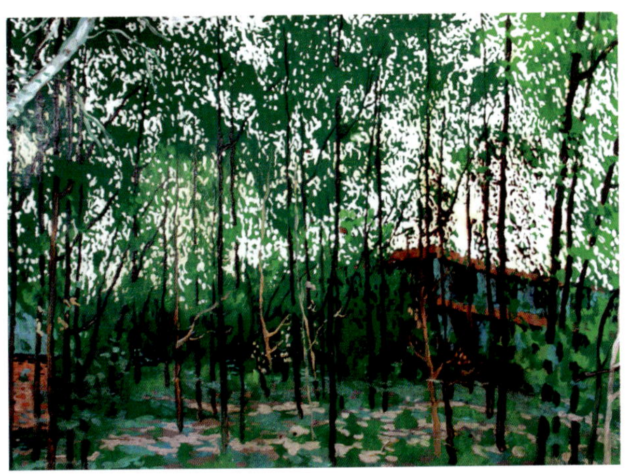

Forest Series
树林系列
2002, Oil on canvas, 40 x 60 cm
2002.002

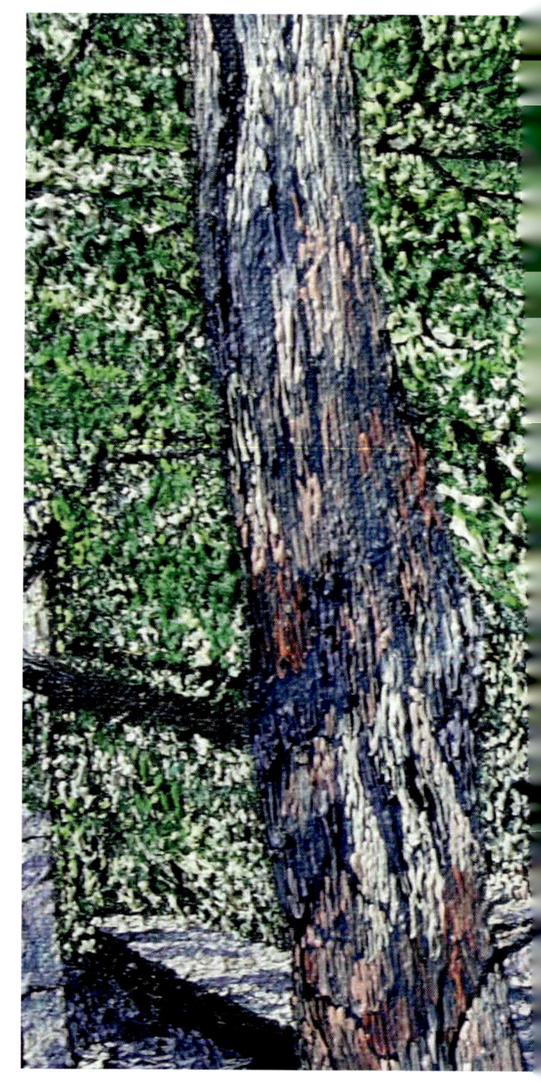

Forest
树林
2002, Oil on canvas, 40 x 50 cm
2002.003

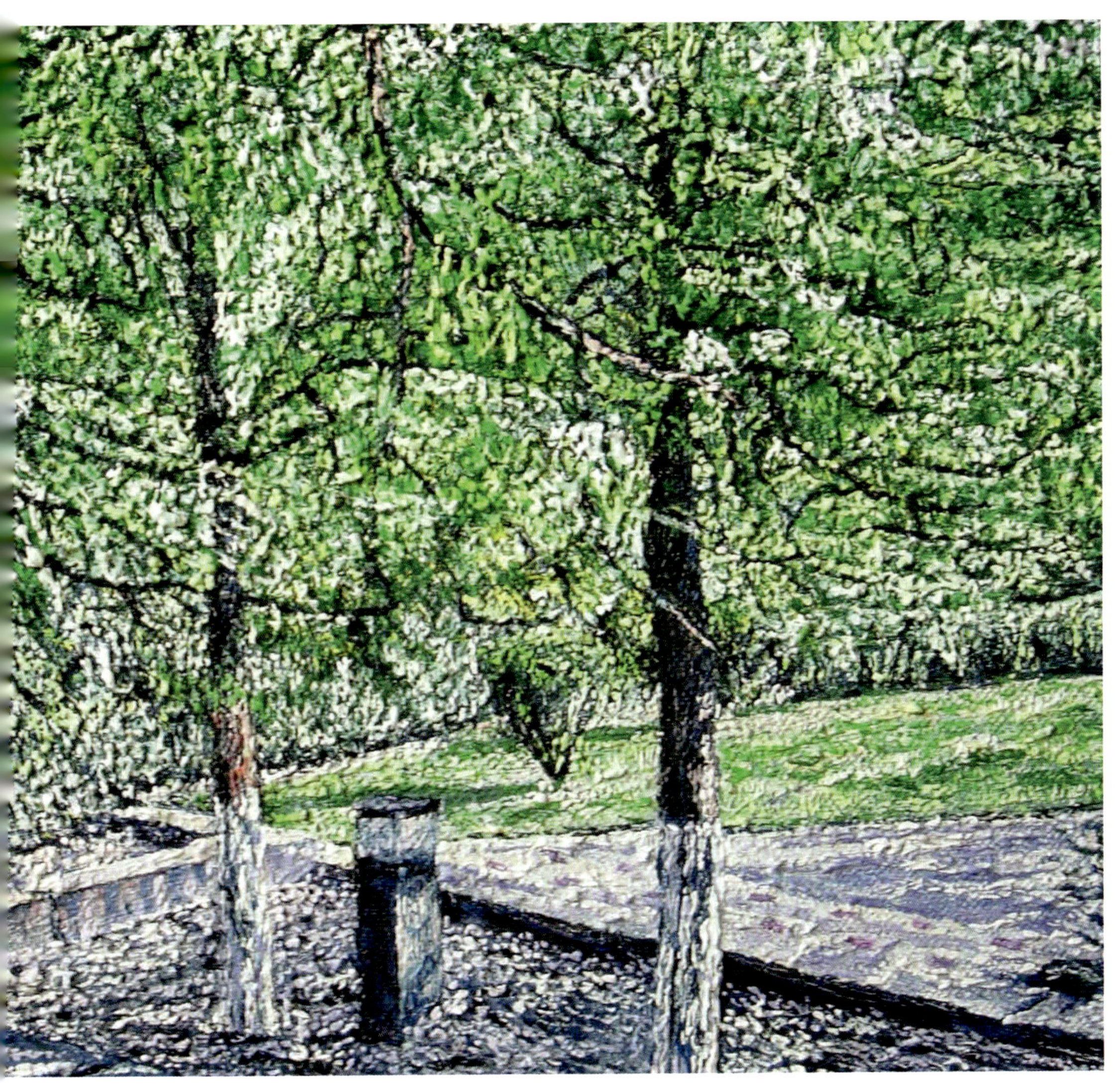

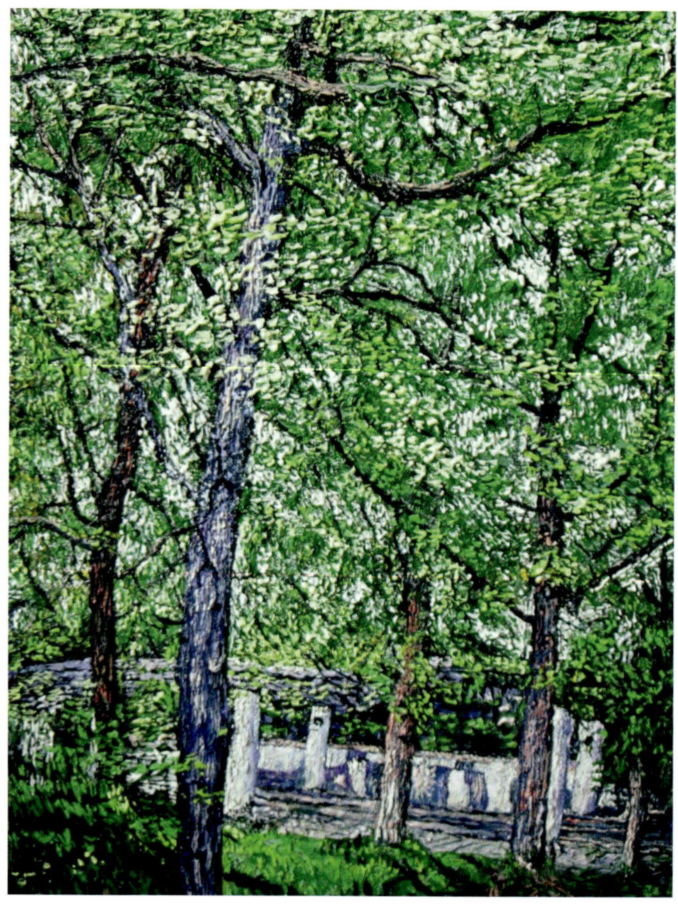

Forest
树林
2002, Oil on canvas, 50 x 40 cm
2002.004

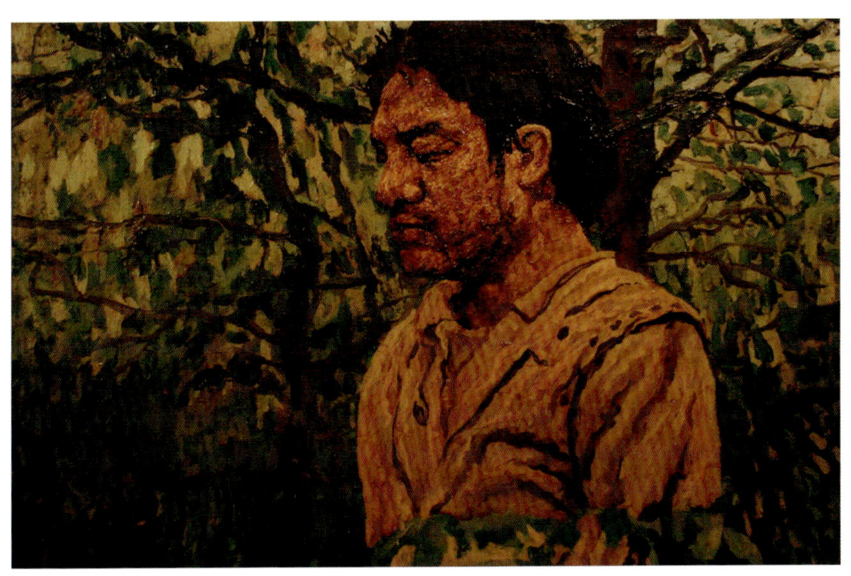

Self-Portrait
自画像
2003, Oil on canvas, 40 x 60 cm
2003.001

Next to Dingshan Reservoir
丁山水库旁
2003, Oil on canvas, 60 x 43 cm
2003.002

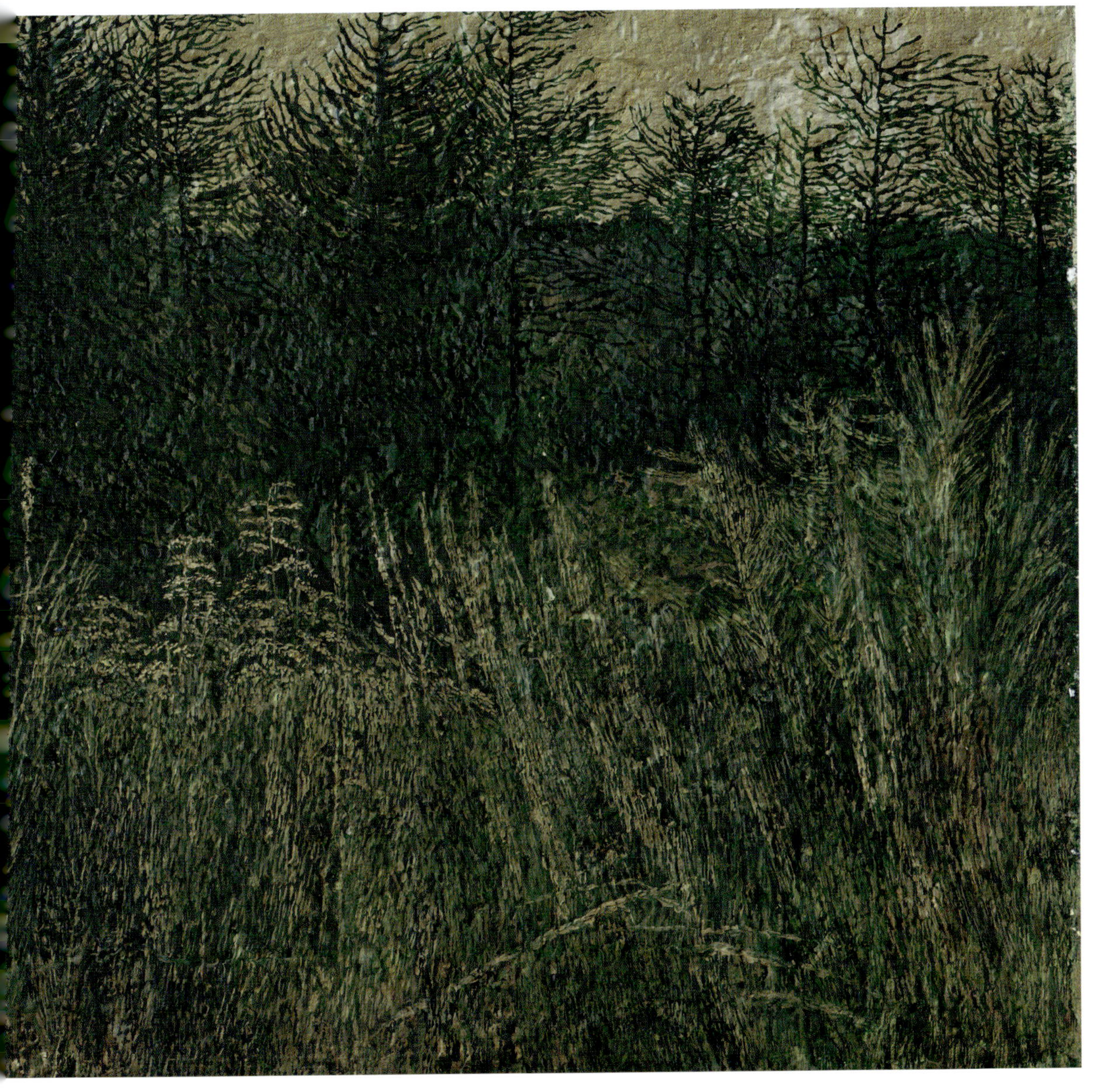

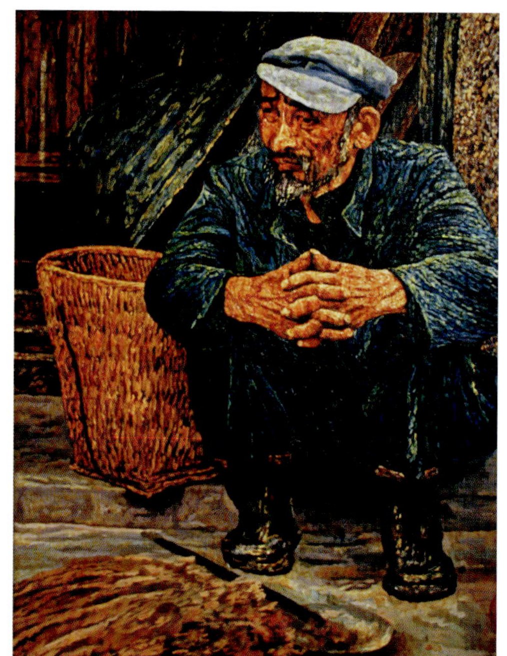

Memories of Dongxi
东溪回忆
2003, Oil on canvas, 70 x 90 cm
2003.003

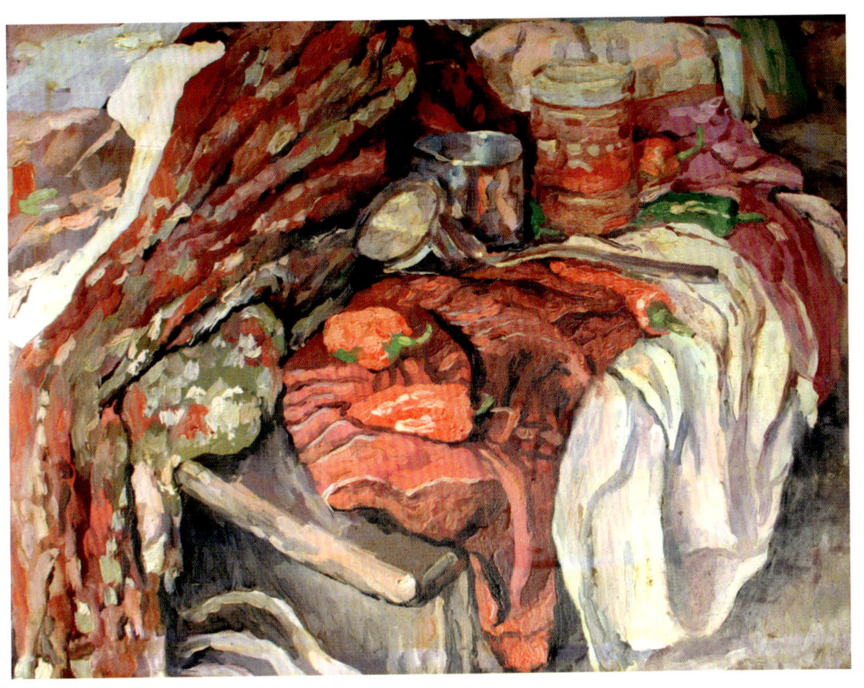

Still Life
静物
2003, Oil on canvas, 30 x 50 cm
2003.004

Mama
妈妈
2003, Oil on canvas, 50 x 70 cm
2003.005

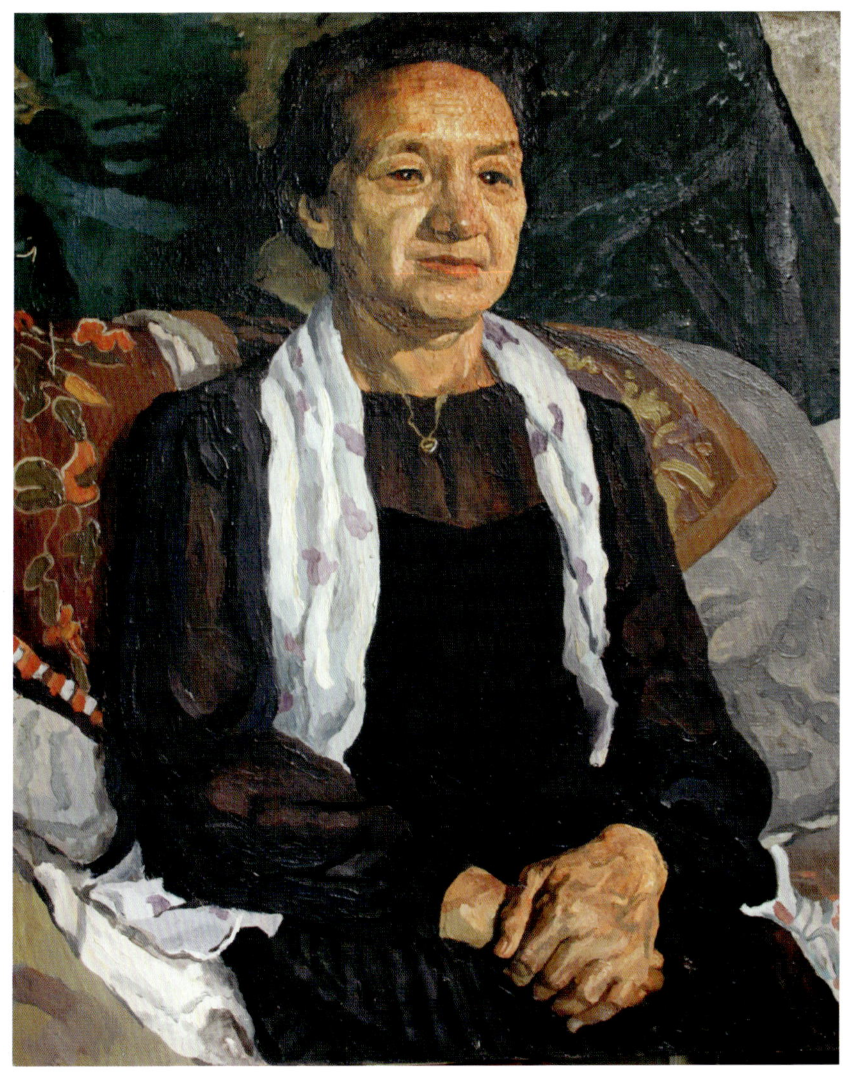

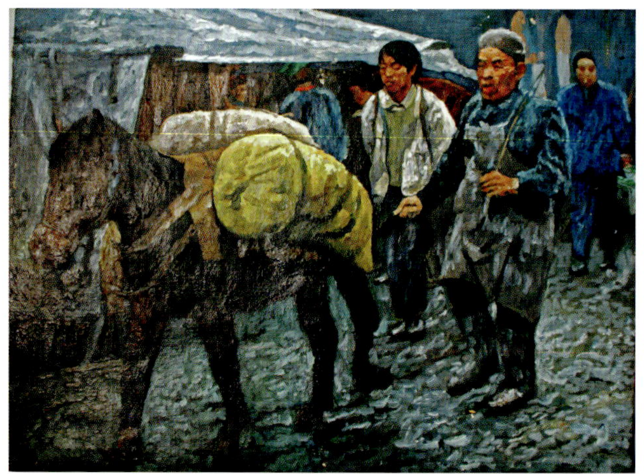

Memories of Dongxi
东溪回忆
2004, Oil on canvas, 100 x 120 cm
2004.001

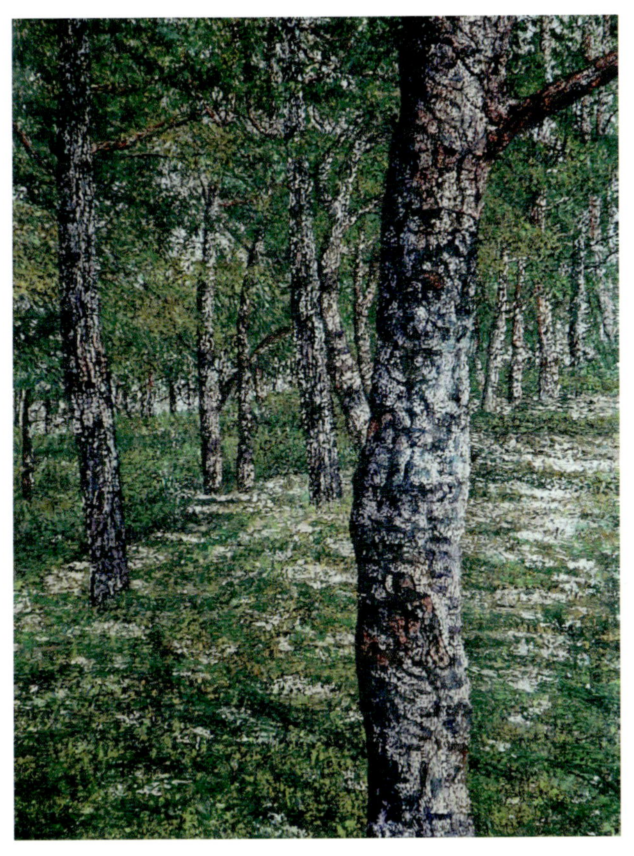

Forest No.3
树林-3
2005, Oil on canvas, 50 x 40 cm
2005.001

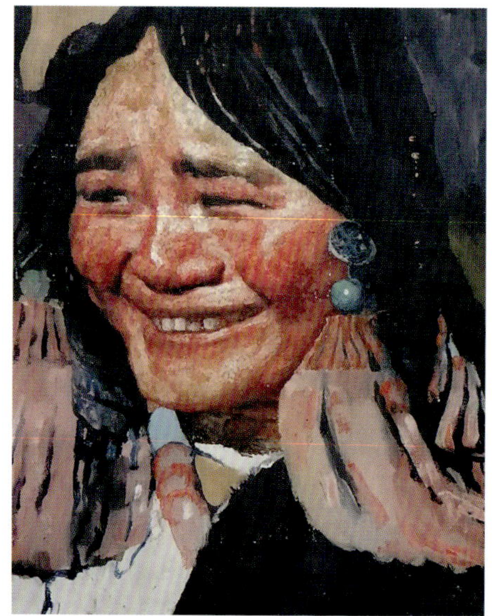

A Tibetan
西藏人
2005, Oil on canvas, 60 x 43 cm
2005.003

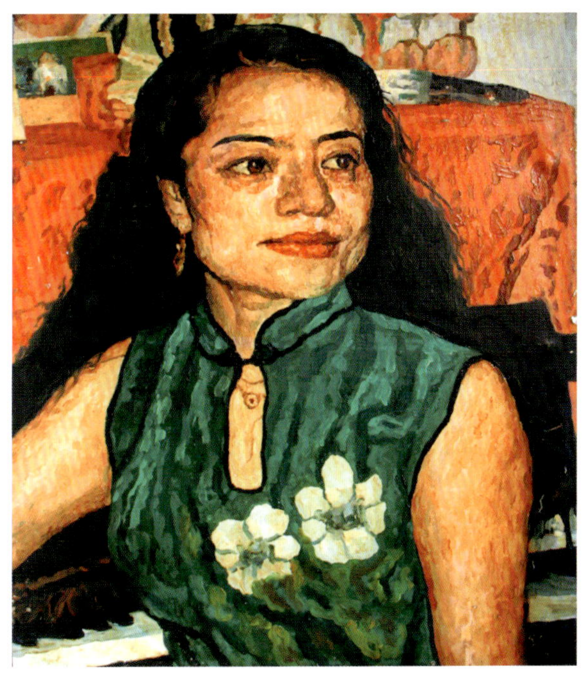

Elder Sister
姐姐
2005, Oil on canvas, 40 x 60 cm
2005.004

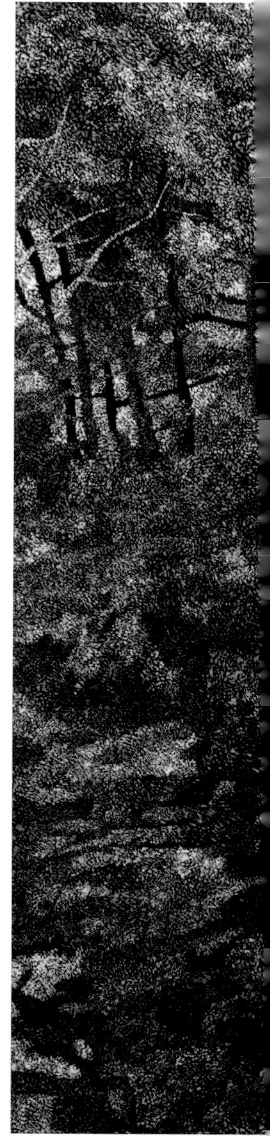

Woods in the Afternoon
下午的树林
2009, Oil on canvas, 80 x 100 cm
2009.001

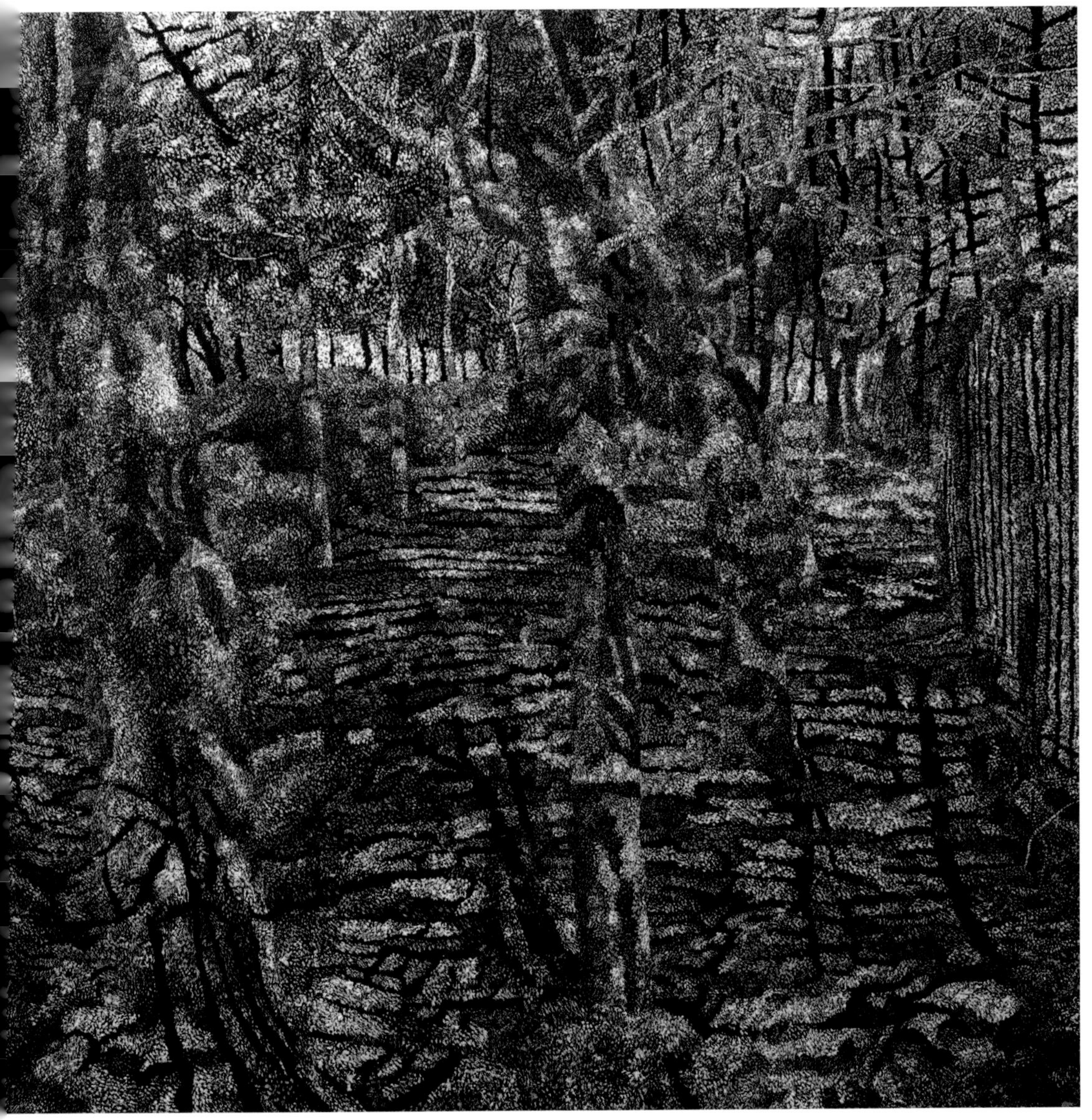

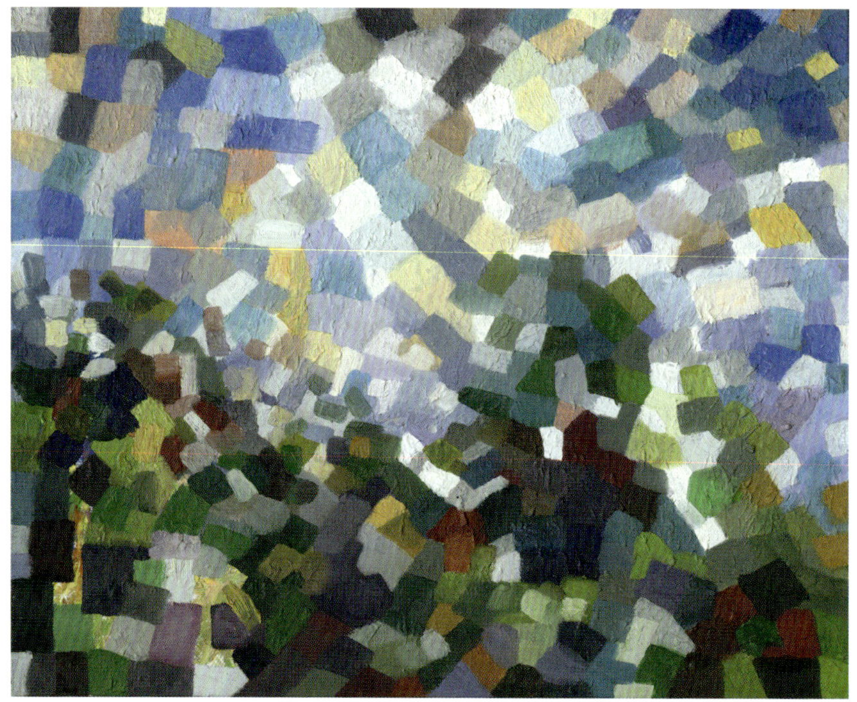

Clouds
云朵
2014, Oil on canvas, 50 x 60 cm
2014.001

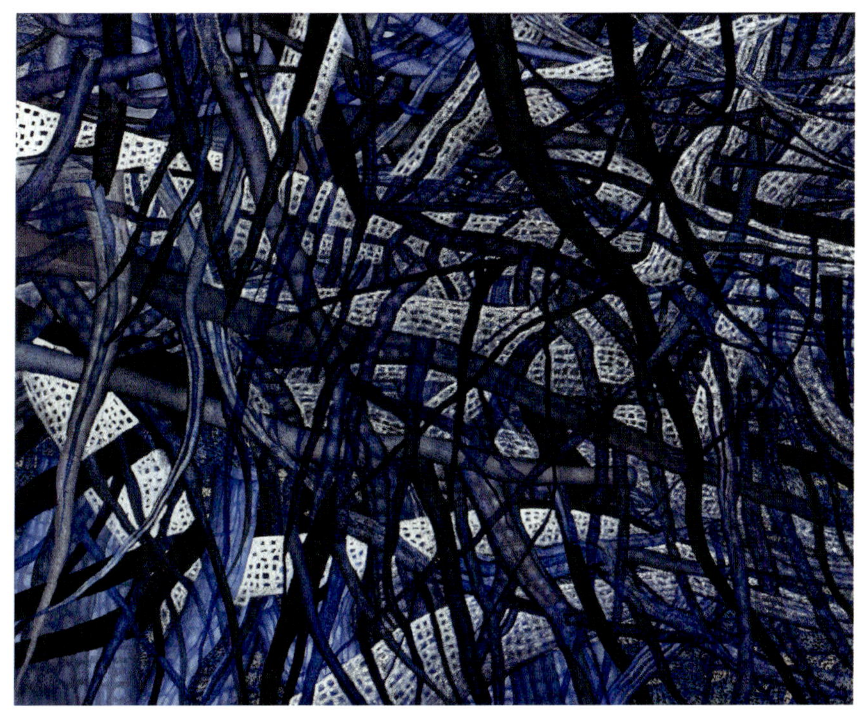

Primitive Grove
原始的树丛
2014, Oil on canvas, 50 x 60 cm
2014.002

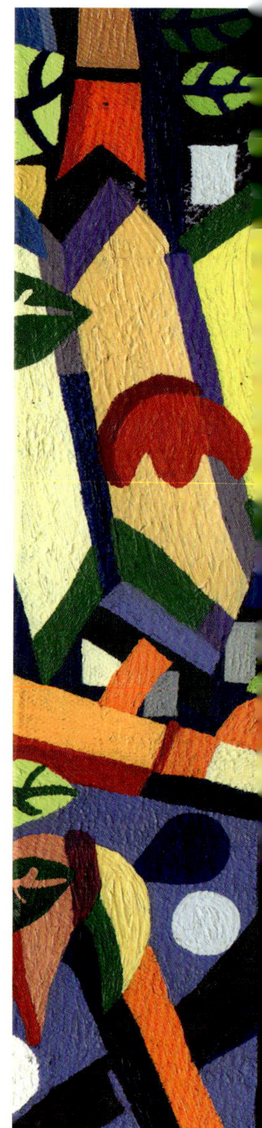

Hometown
家乡
2014, Oil on canvas, 40 x 50 cm
2014.003

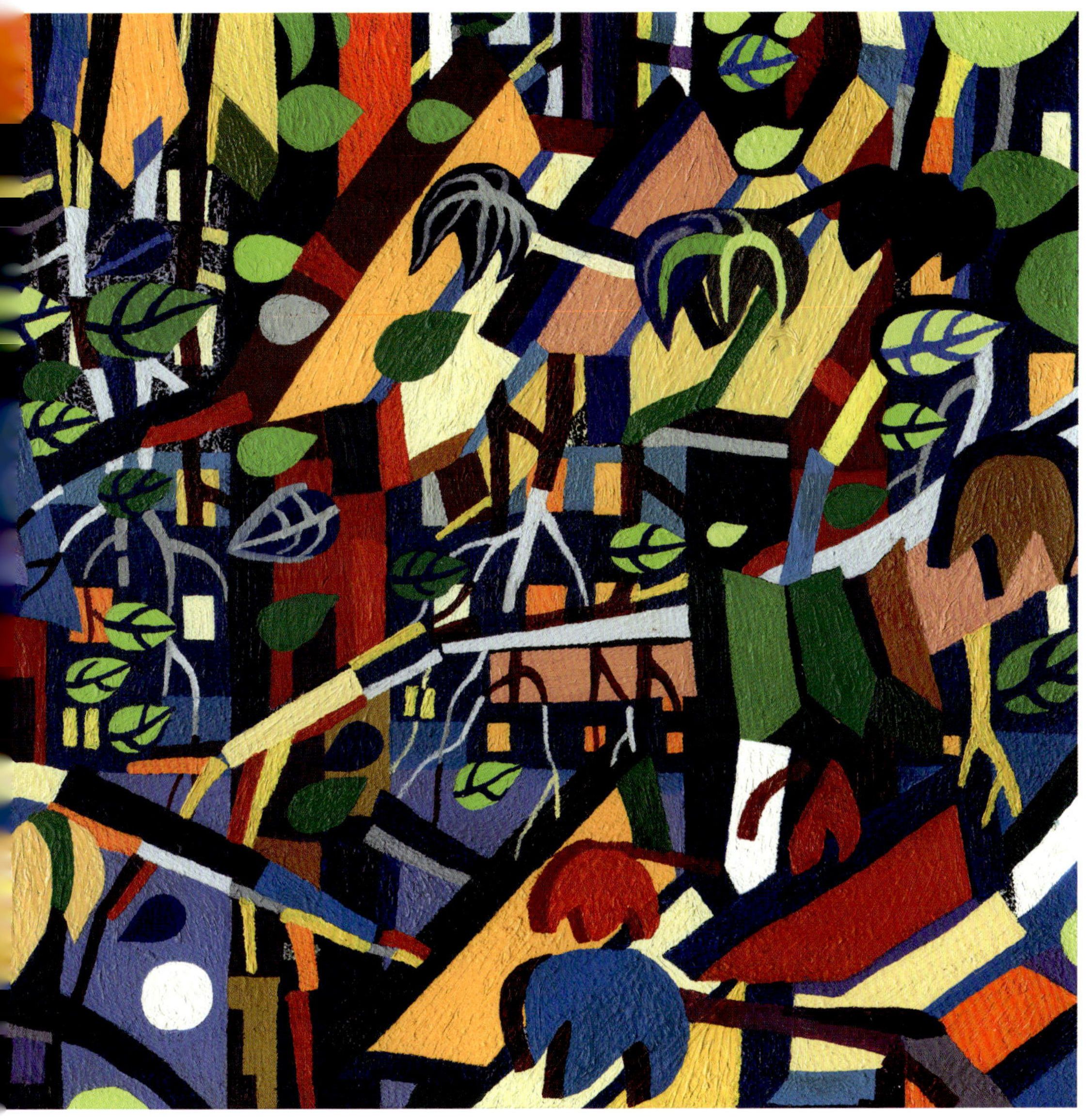

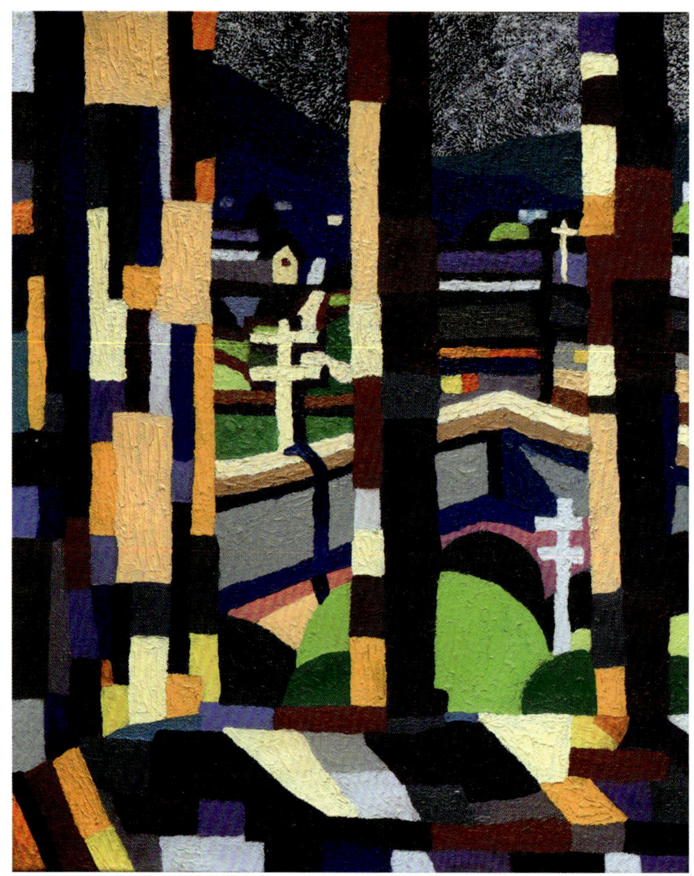

Hometown No. 2
家乡 2
2014, Oil on canvas, 45 x 35 cm
2014.004

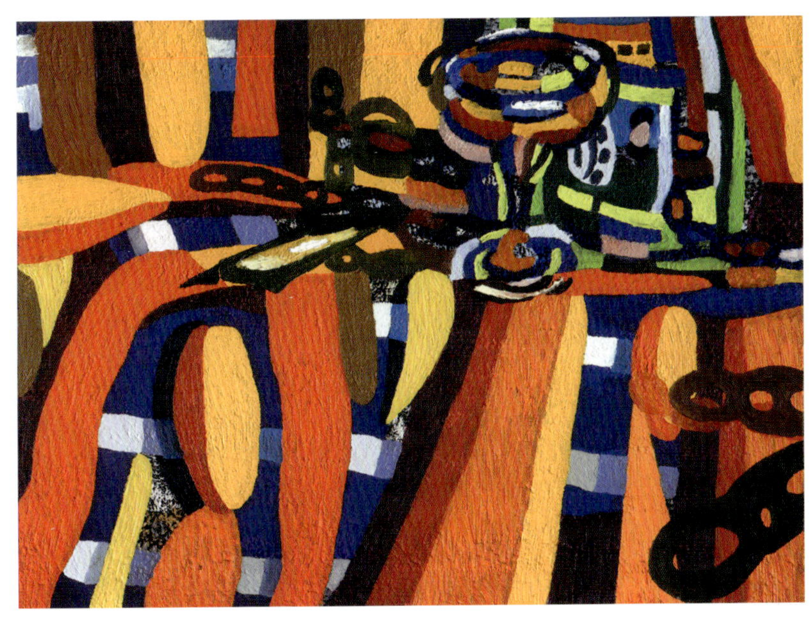

Still Life in the Studio
画室里的静物
2014, Oil on canvas, 30 x 40 cm
2014.005

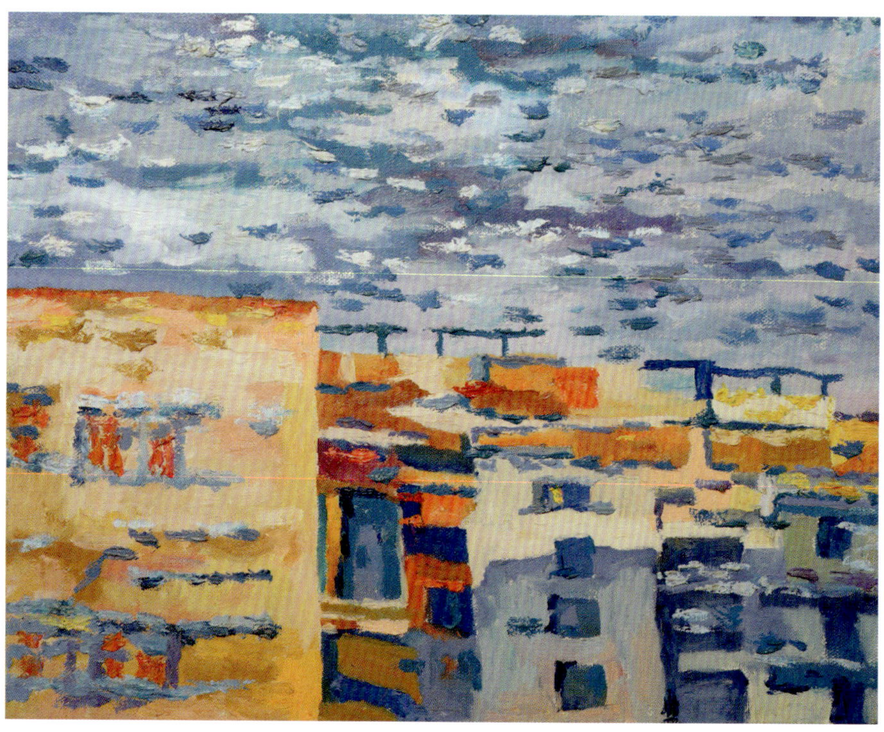

The Big Sun Outside the Window
窗外的大太阳
2015, Oil on canvas, 45 x 55 cm
2015.002

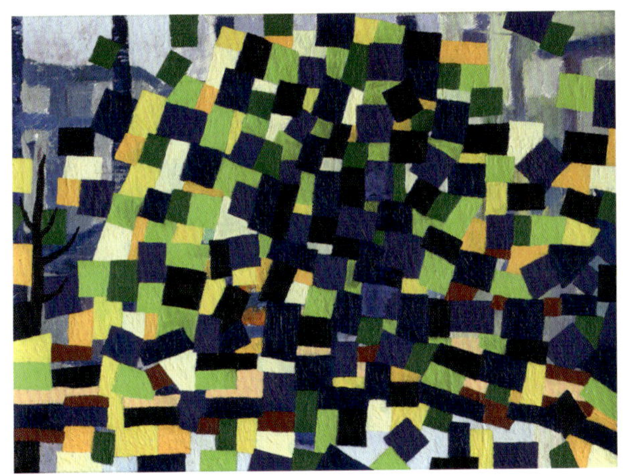

Dongxi Rice Field
东溪稻田
2015, Oil on canvas, 30 x 40 cm
2015.003

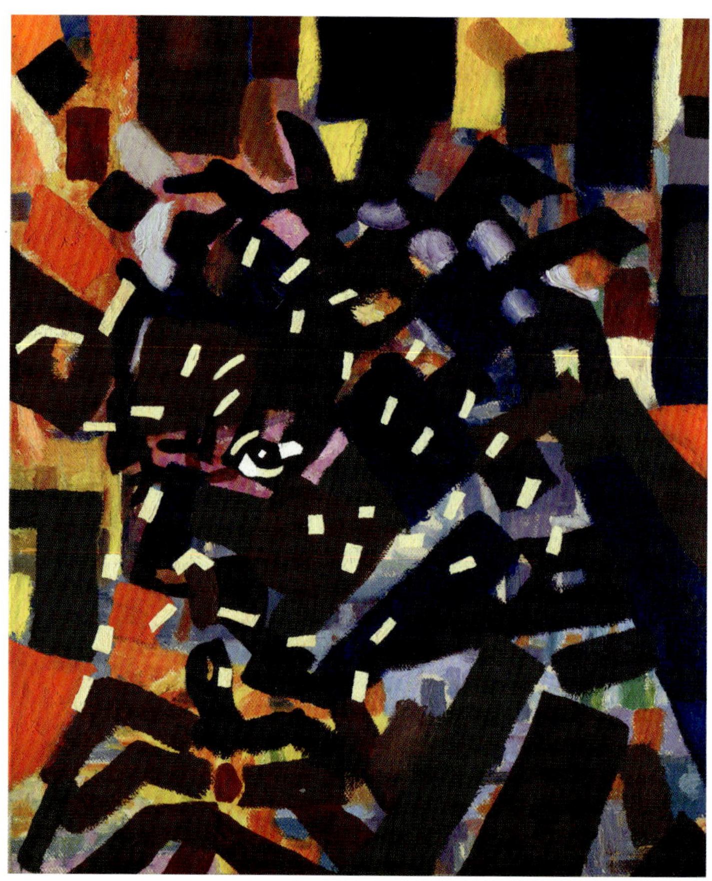

Figure
人像
2015, Oil on canvas, 55 x 45 cm
2015.004

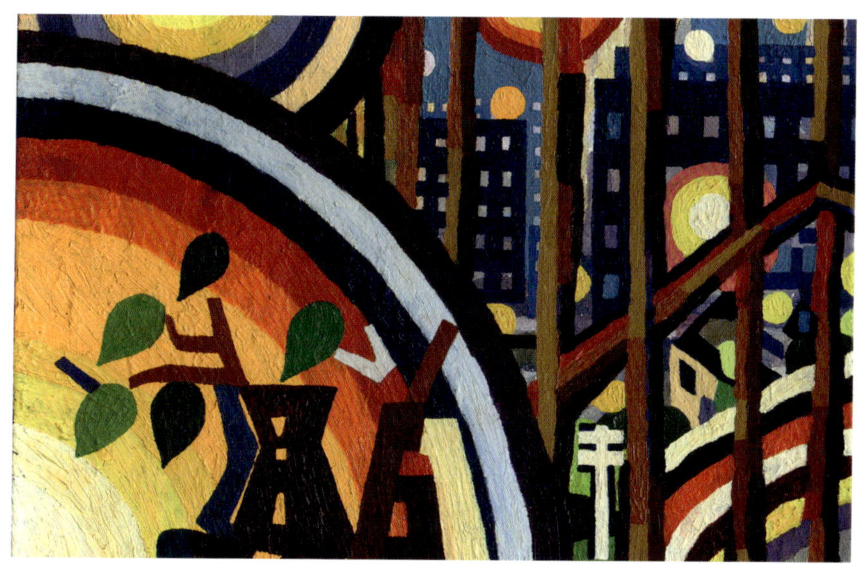

City Light
城市的光
2015, Oil on canvas, 30 x 40 cm
2015.005

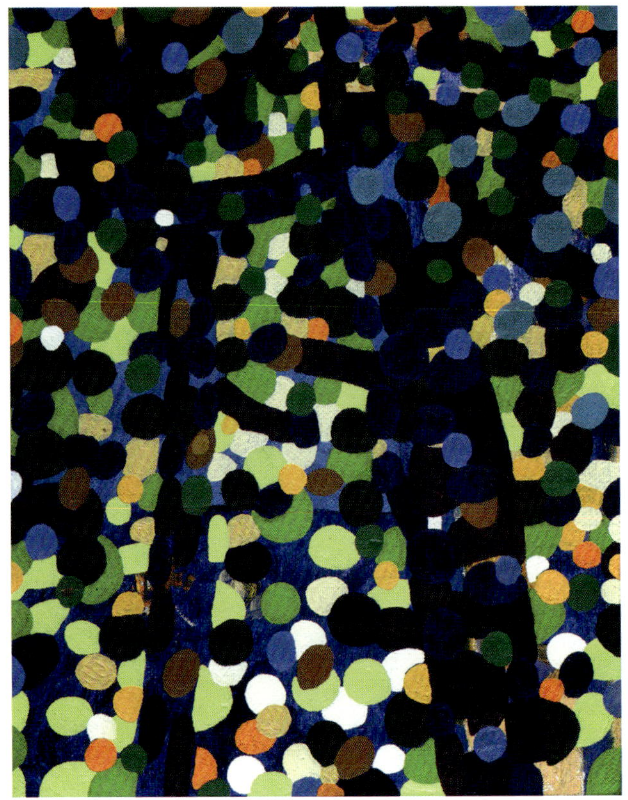

Backlit Woods
逆光的树林
2015, Oil on canvas, 40 x 30 cm
2015.006

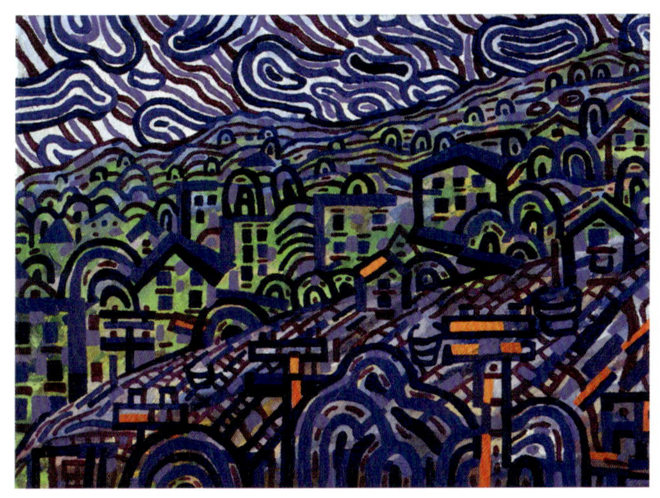

Liujiang, Sichuan
四川柳江
2016, Oil on canvas, 30 x 40 cm
2016.001

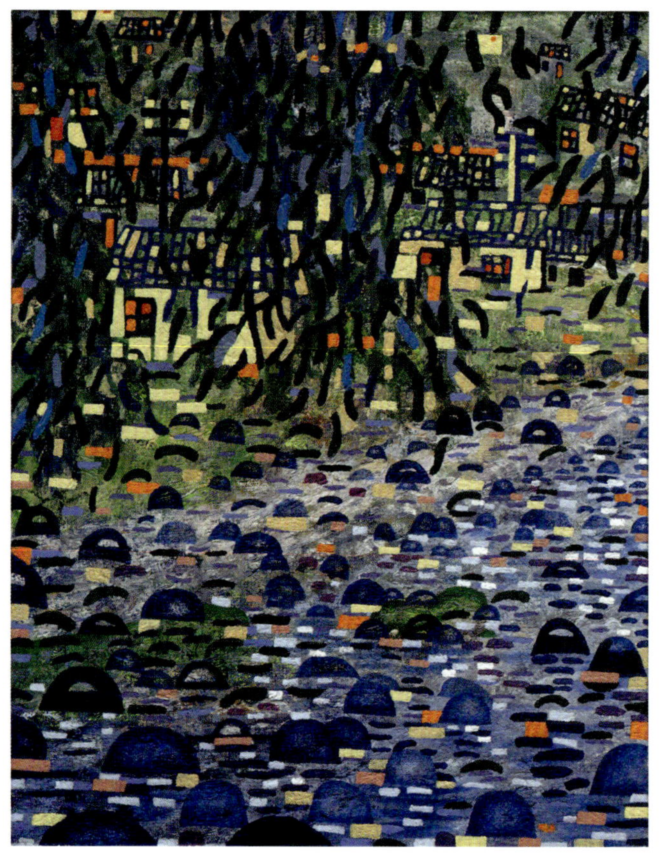

Dongxi Creek
东溪小河
2016, Oil on canvas, 40 x 30 cm
2016.002

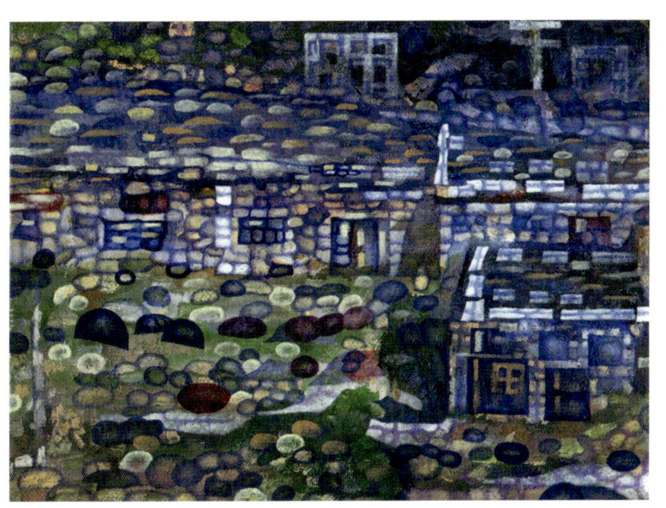

Dongxi Farm Pig Pen
东溪农场猪圈
2016, Oil on canvas, 30 x 40 cm
2016.004

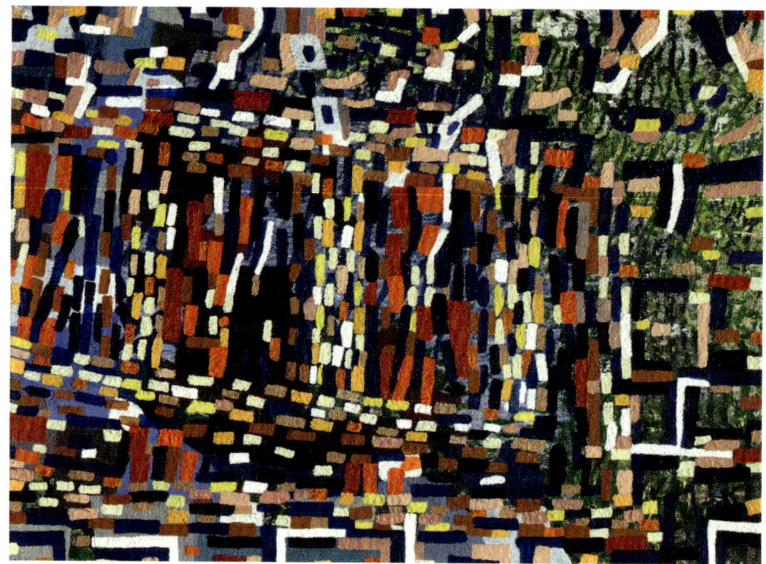

Basement Window
地下室的窗口
2016, Oil on canvas, 30 x 40 cm
2016.005

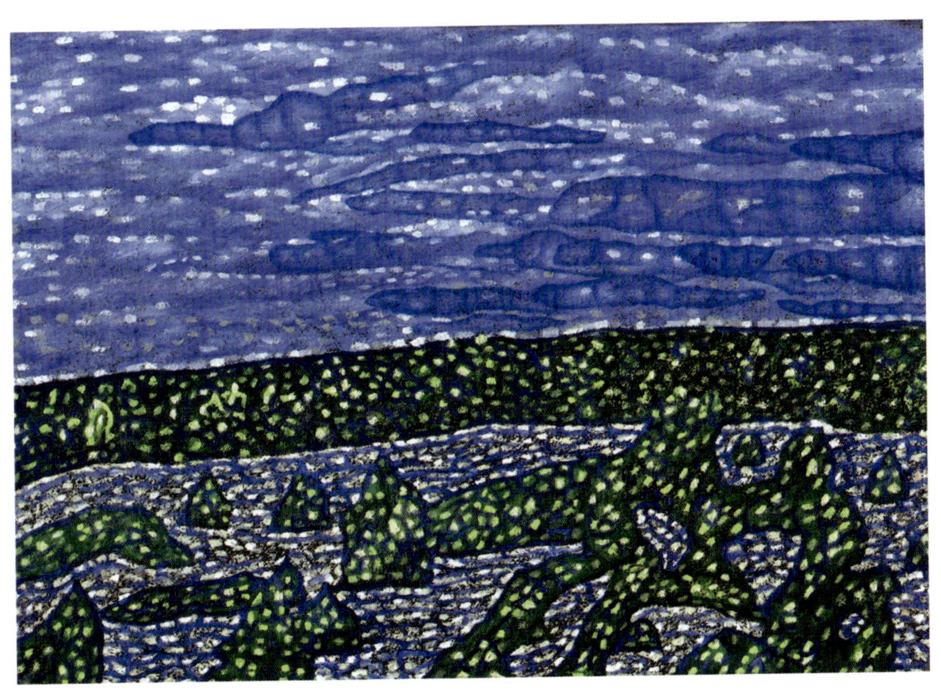

Open Space
开阔地
2016, Oil on canvas, 25 x 35 cm
2016.006

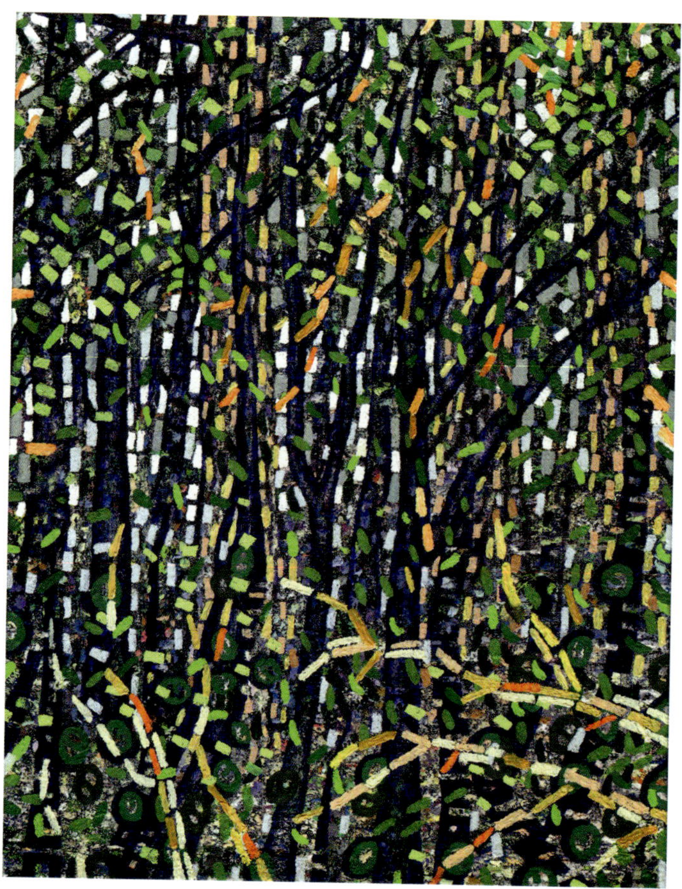

Chengdu Botanical Garden
成都植物园
2016, Oil on canvas, 40 x 30 cm
2016.007

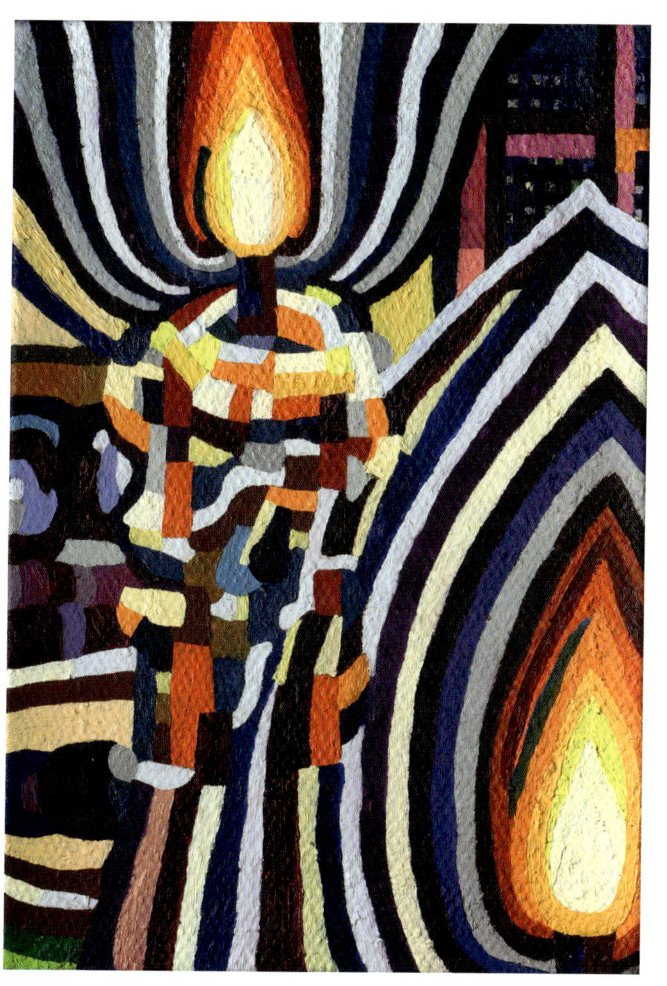

Burning Candles
燃烧的蜡烛
2016, Oil on canvas, 30 x 20 cm
2016.008

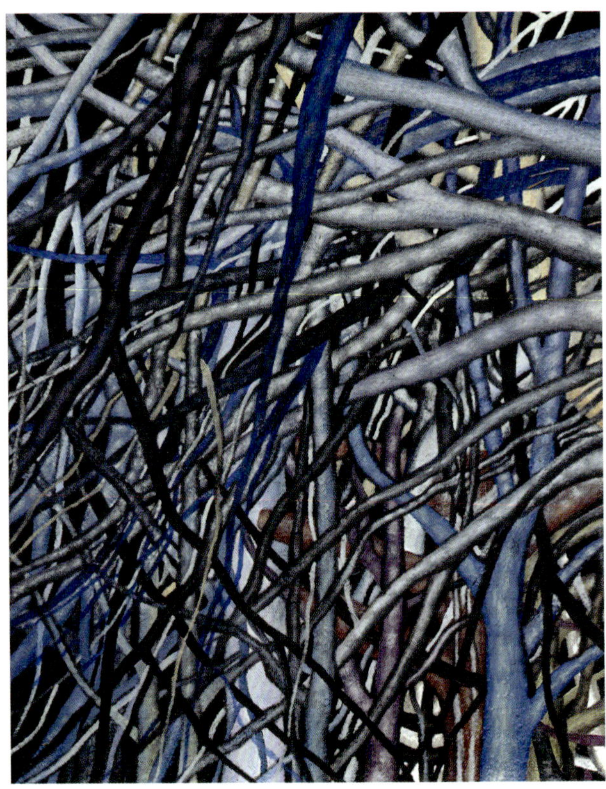

Tangled Branches
缠绕的树枝
2016, Oil on canvas, 40 x 30 cm
2016.009

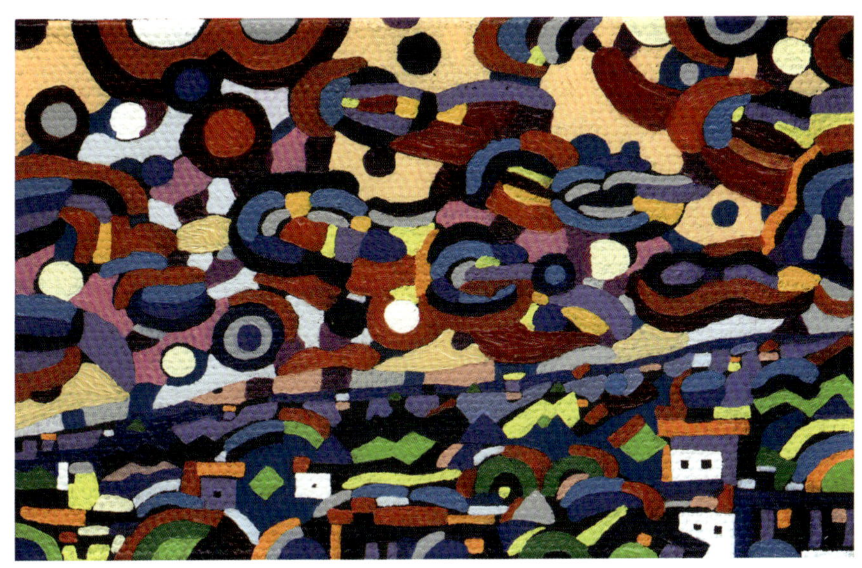

Dongxi sunset
东溪晚霞
2016, Oil on canvas, 20 x 30 cm
2016.010

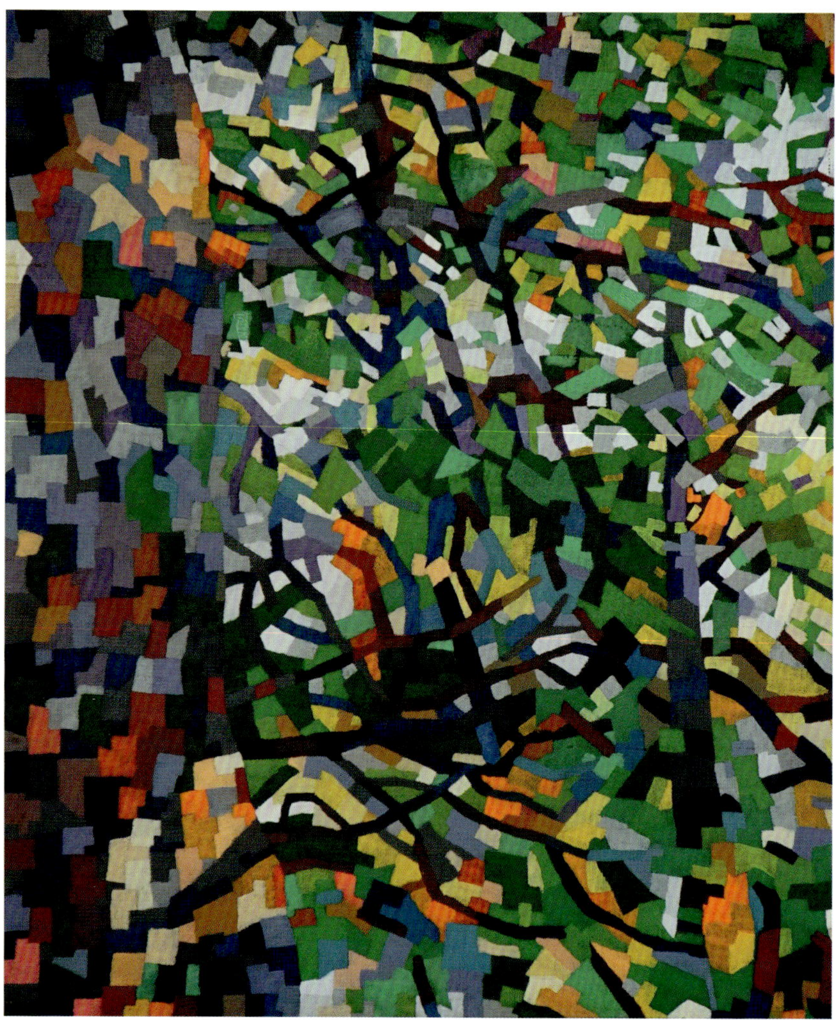

Colorful Leaves
斑斓的树叶
2017, Oil on canvas, 100 x 80 cm
2017.002

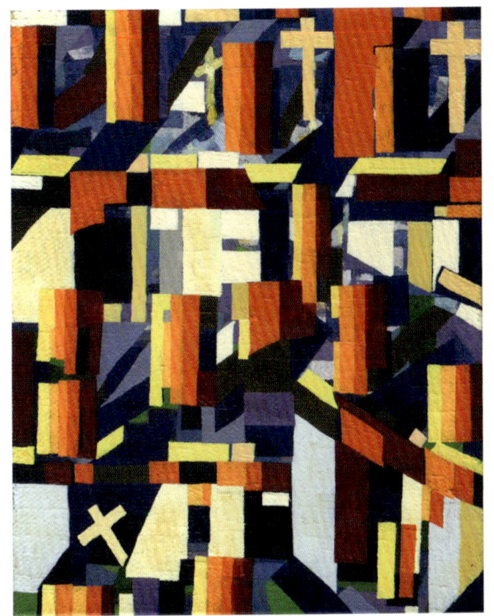

Memories No. 9
回忆 9
2017, Oil on canvas, 40 x 30 cm
2017.004

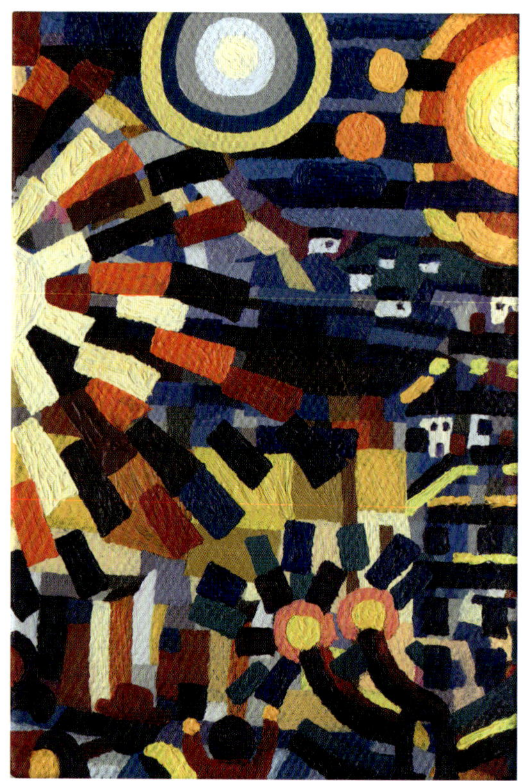

Night Light
夜晚的光
2017, Oil on canvas, 30 x 20 cm
2017.005

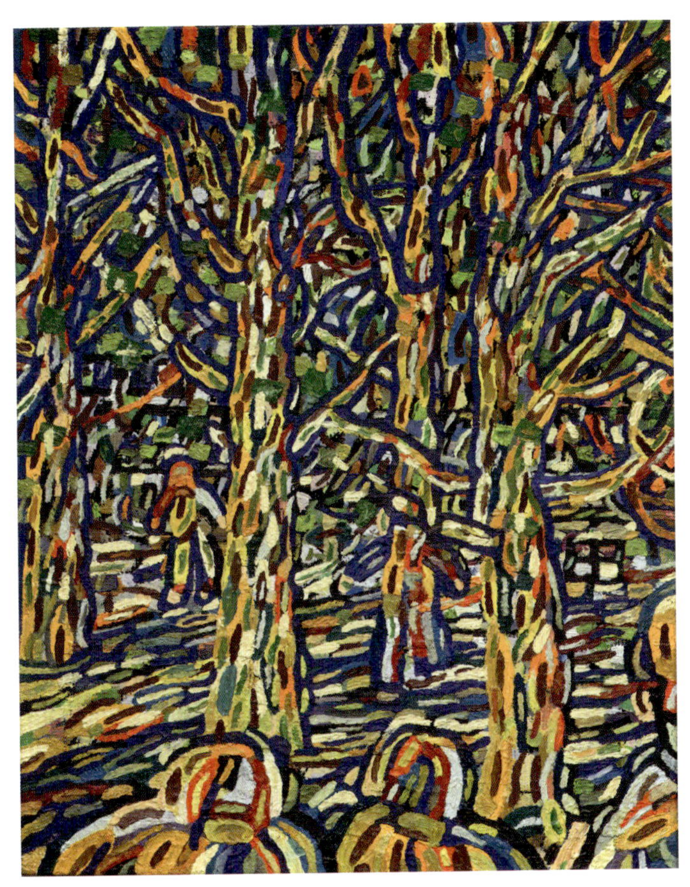

A Park in Midsummer
盛夏的公园
2017, Oil on canvas, 40 x 30 cm
2017.006

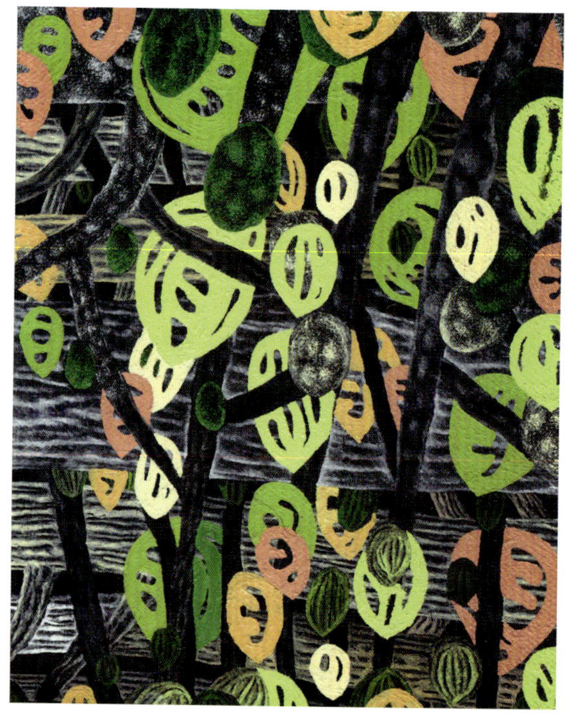

Green Branches
绿色树枝
2017, Oil on canvas, 40 x 30 cm
2017.007

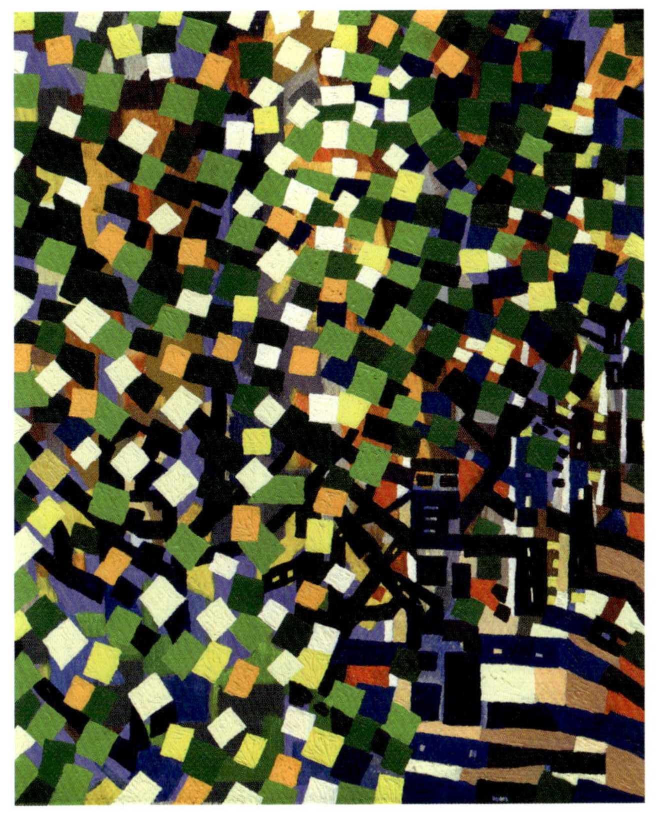

Roadside
路边
2017, Oil on canvas, 45 x 35 cm
2017.008

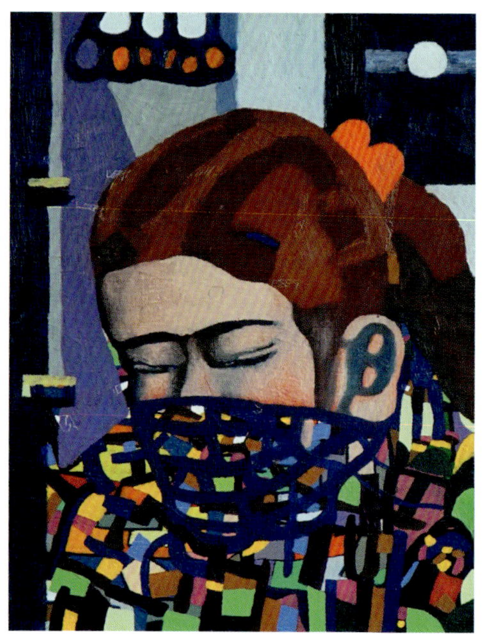

Little Girl on the Subway
地铁上的小女孩
2017, Oil on canvas, 40 x 30 cm
2017.009

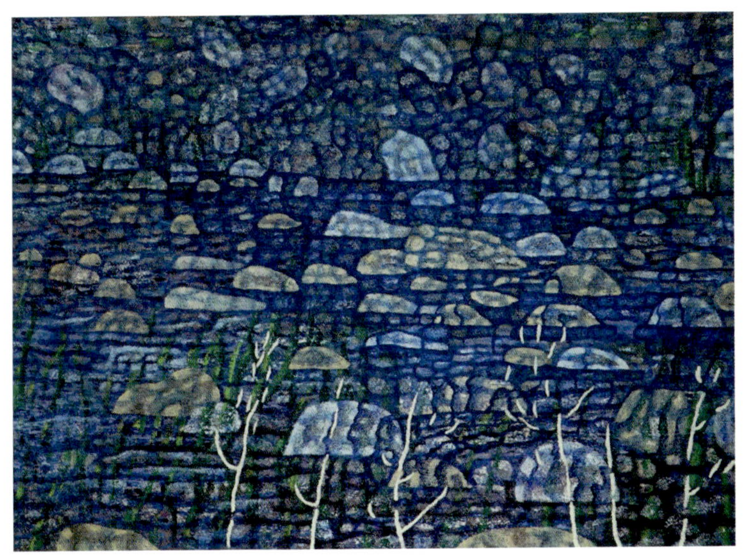

River with Stones
有石头的河
2018, Oil on canvas, 30 x 40 cm
2018.001

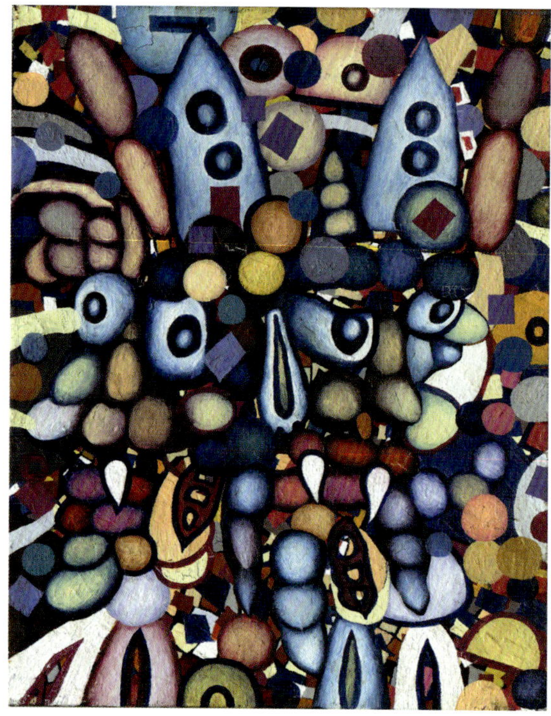

Imagination
想象
2018, Oil on canvas, 45 x 35 cm
2018.002

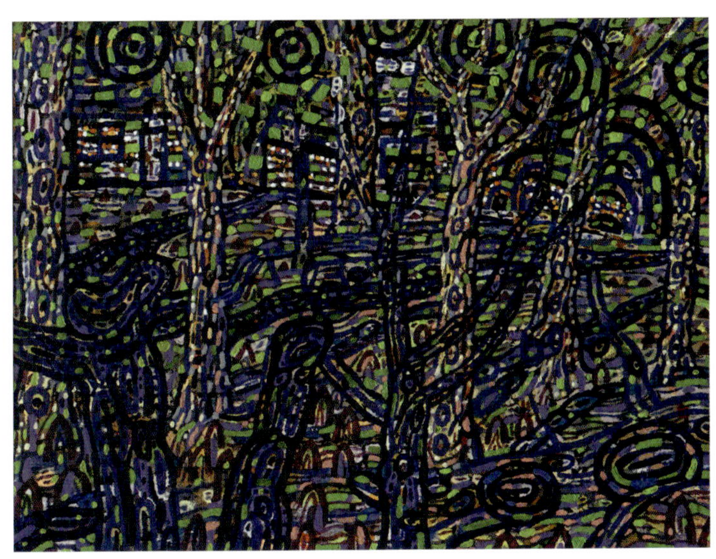

Roadside Bushes
路边树丛
2018, Oil on canvas, 35 x 45 cm
2018.003

Night at Dongxi Farm
东溪农场的夜晚
2018, Oil on canvas, 100 x 80 cm
2018.004

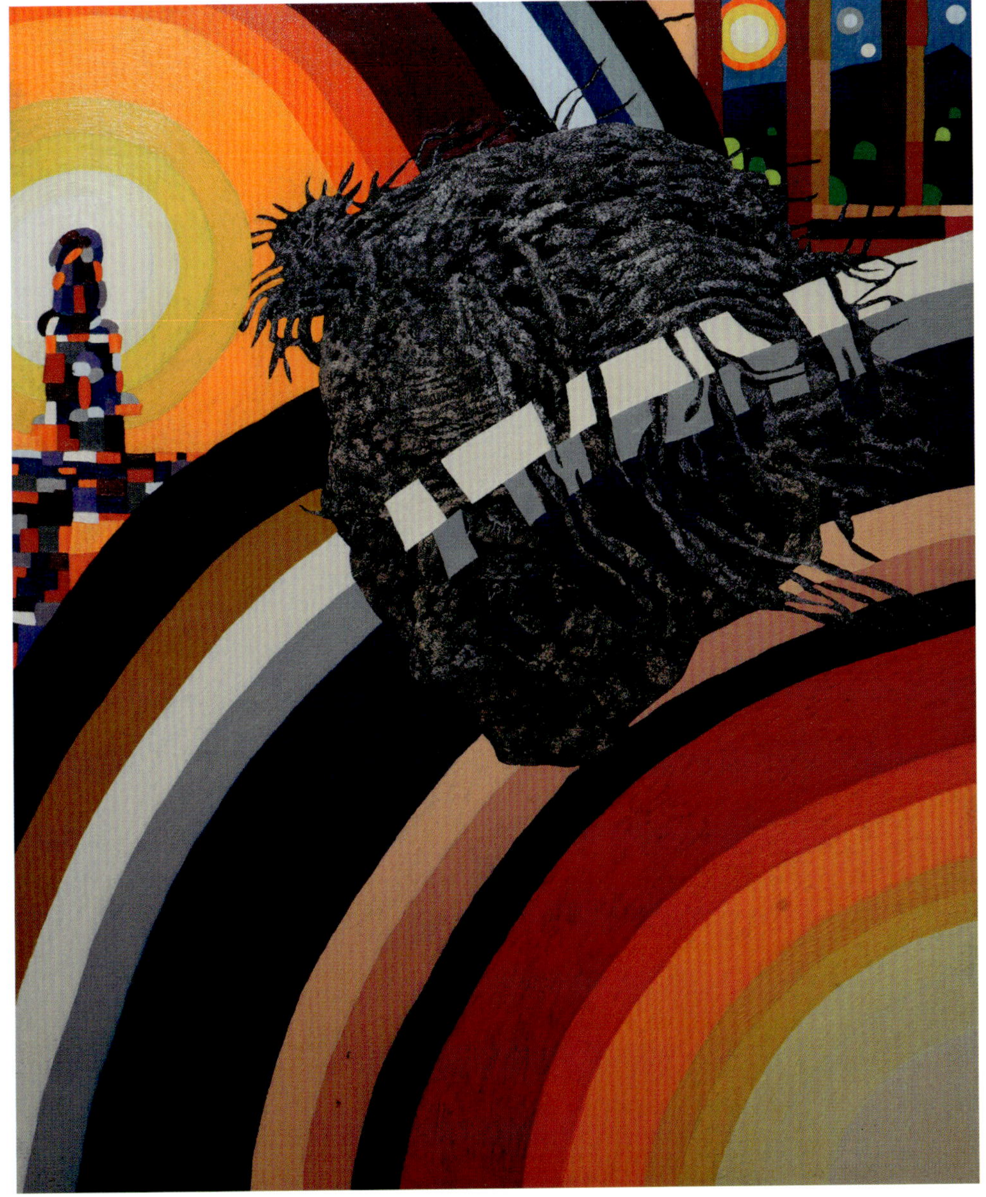

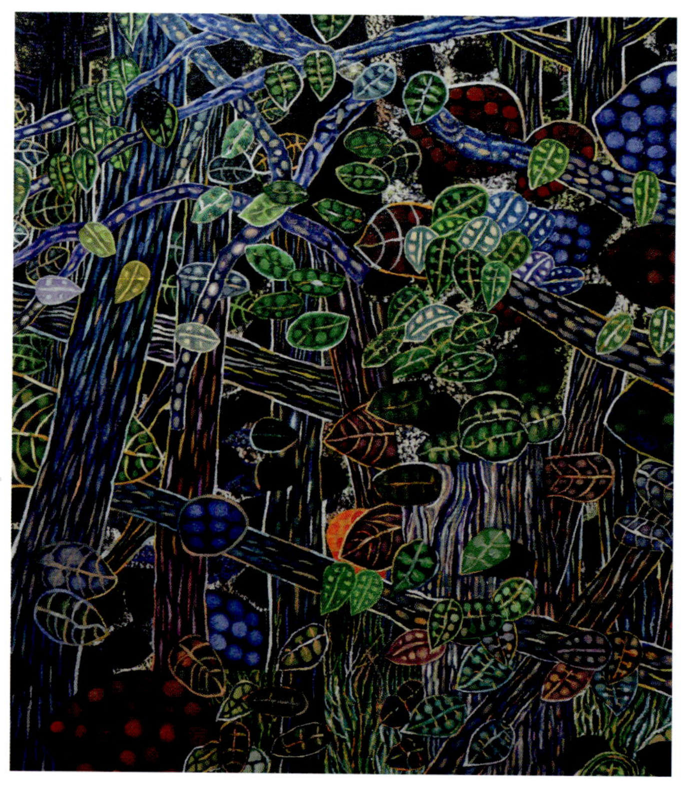

Fantasy Tree
幻想的树
2018, Oil on canvas, 70 x 60 cm
2018.006

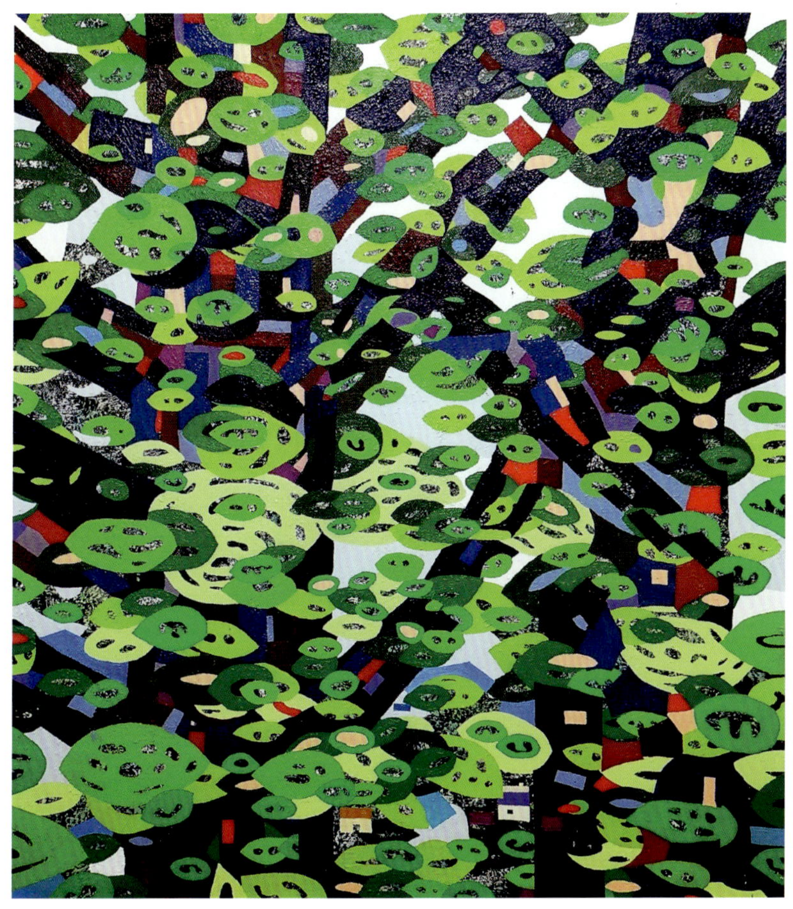

Spring Leaves
春天的树叶
2018, Oil on canvas, 85 x 70 cm
2018.009

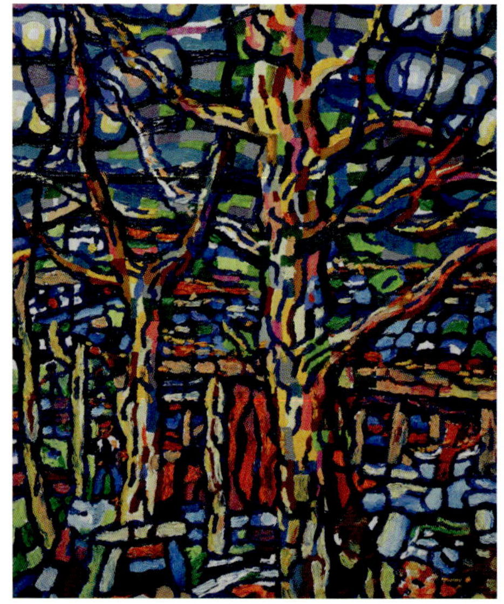

A Place in Dongxi
东溪下场口
2019, Oil on canvas, 30 x 24 cm
2019.001

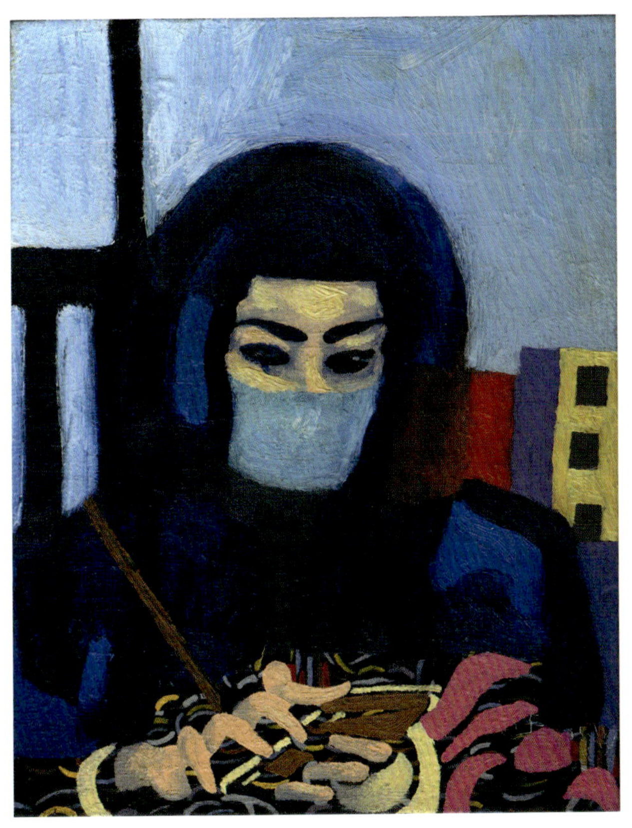

On the Bus
公交车上
2019, Oil on canvas, 40 x 30 cm
2019.002

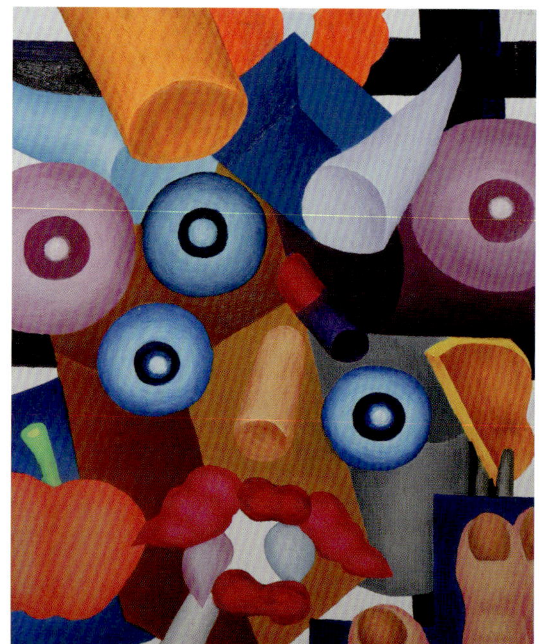

People in Shopping Mall
商场里的人
2019, Oil on canvas, 50 x 40 cm
2019.003

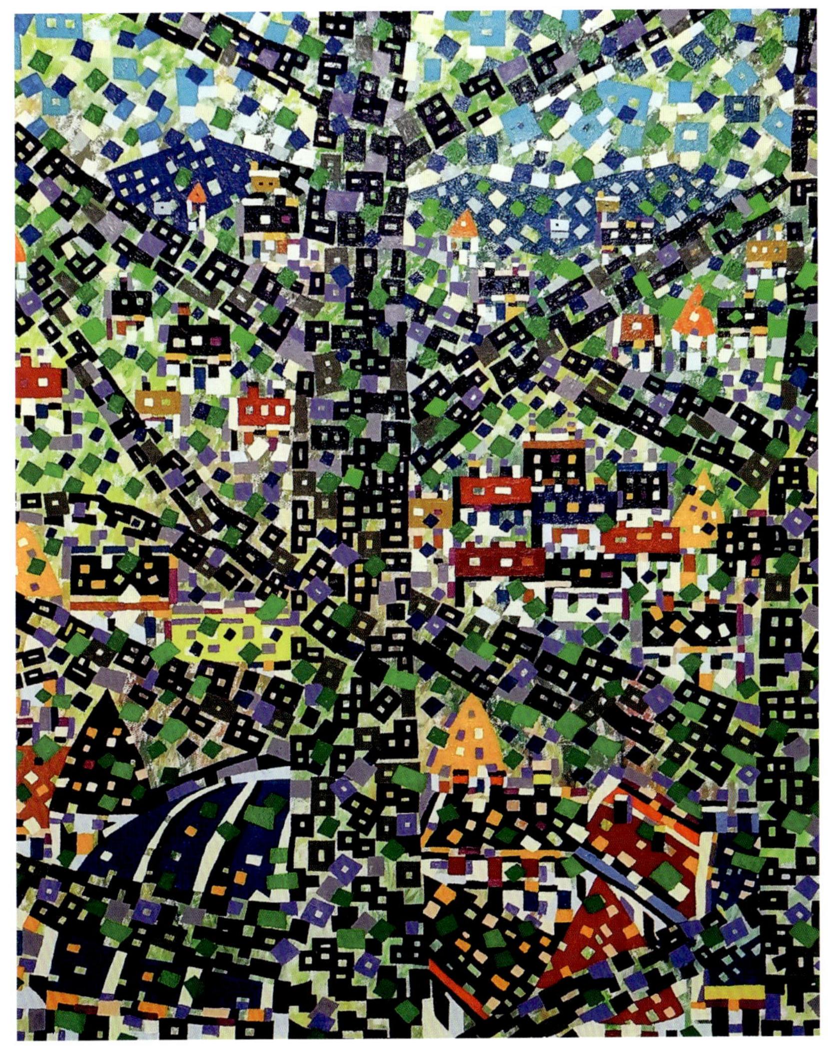

European Woods
欧洲树林
2019, Oil on canvas, 80 x 60 cm
2019.004

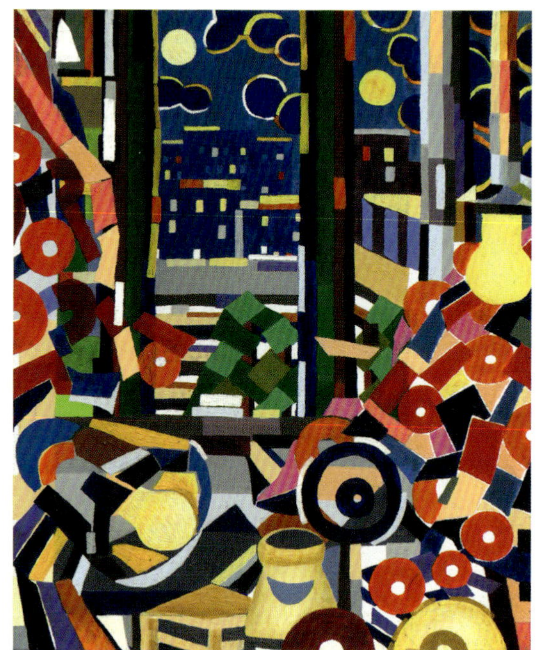

Memories No. 8
回忆 8
2019, Oil on canvas, 50 x 40 cm
2019.005

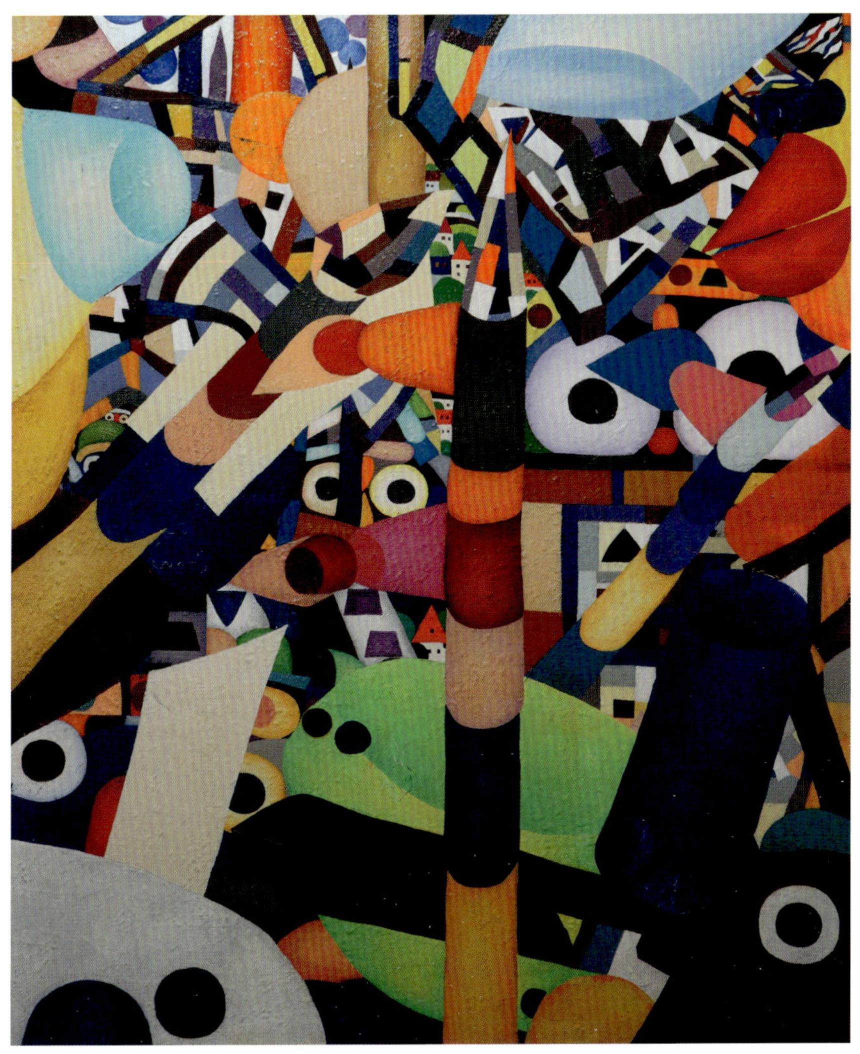

Ancient European Battlefields
欧洲古战场
2019, Oil on canvas, 80 x 100 cm
2019.007

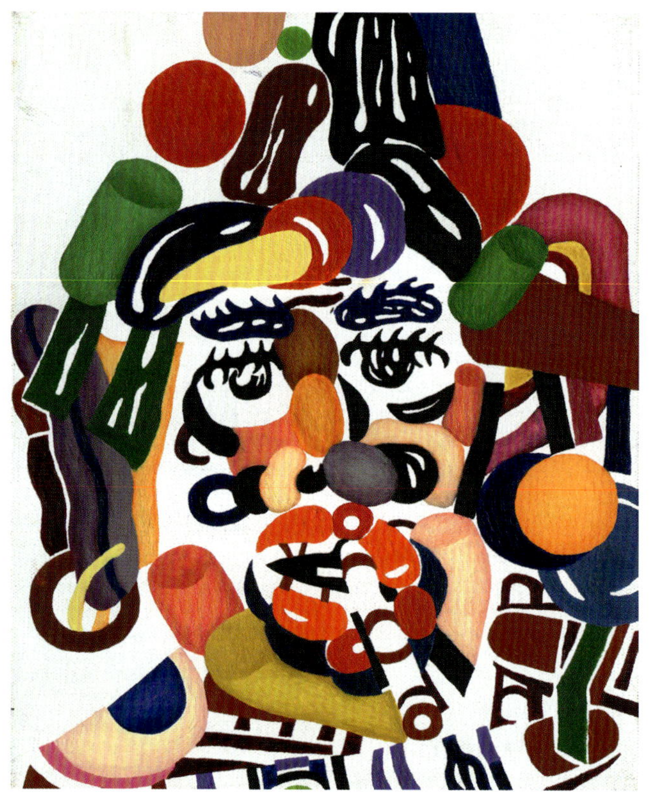

A Clown
小丑
2019, Oil on canvas, 50 x 40 cm
2019.010

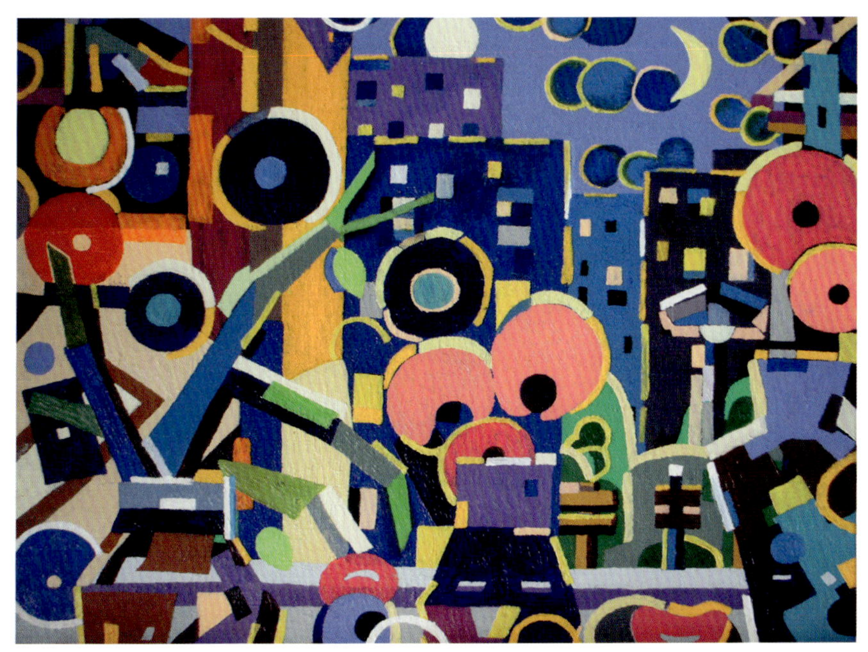

Rear Window
后窗
2019, Oil on canvas, 40 x 50 cm
2019.011

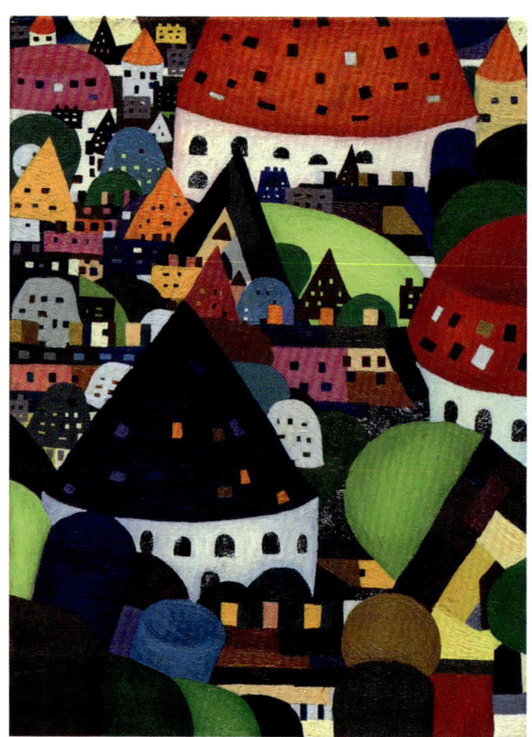

Memories European Impressions No. 4
回忆 欧洲印象 4
2020, Oil on canvas, 35 x 25 cm
2020.003

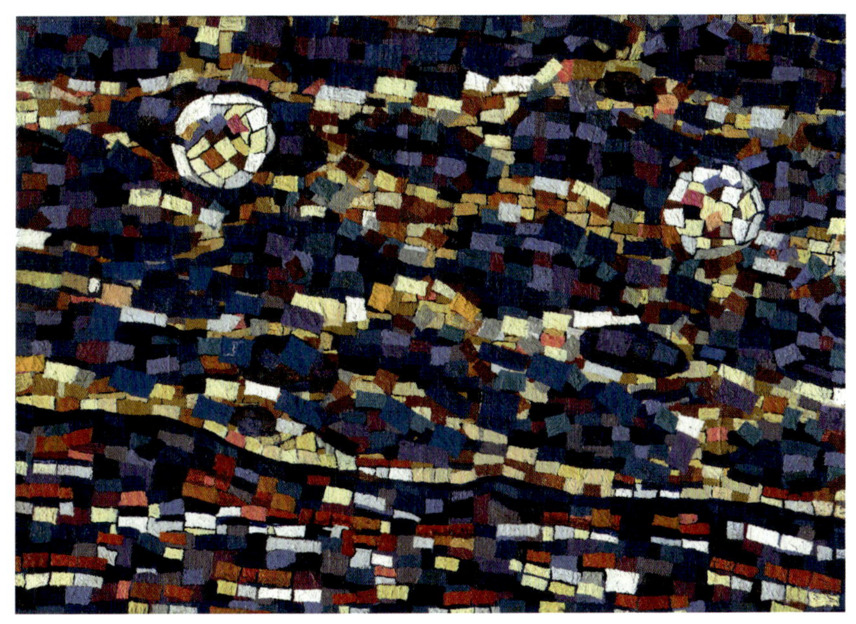

The Sun
太阳
2020, Oil on canvas, 35 x 25 cm
2020.004

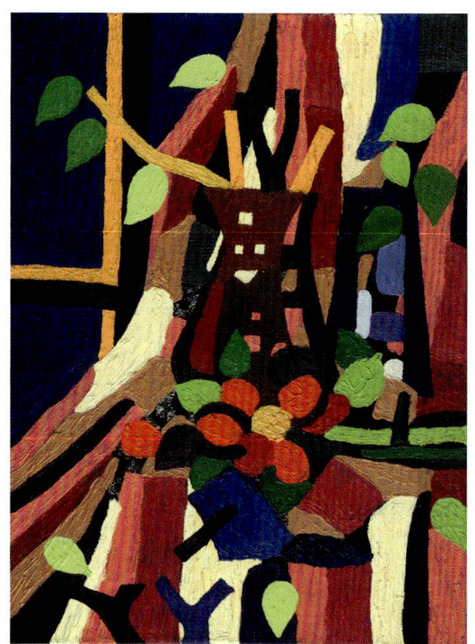

In Front of the Window
窗前
2020, Oil on canvas, 35 x 25 cm
2020.005

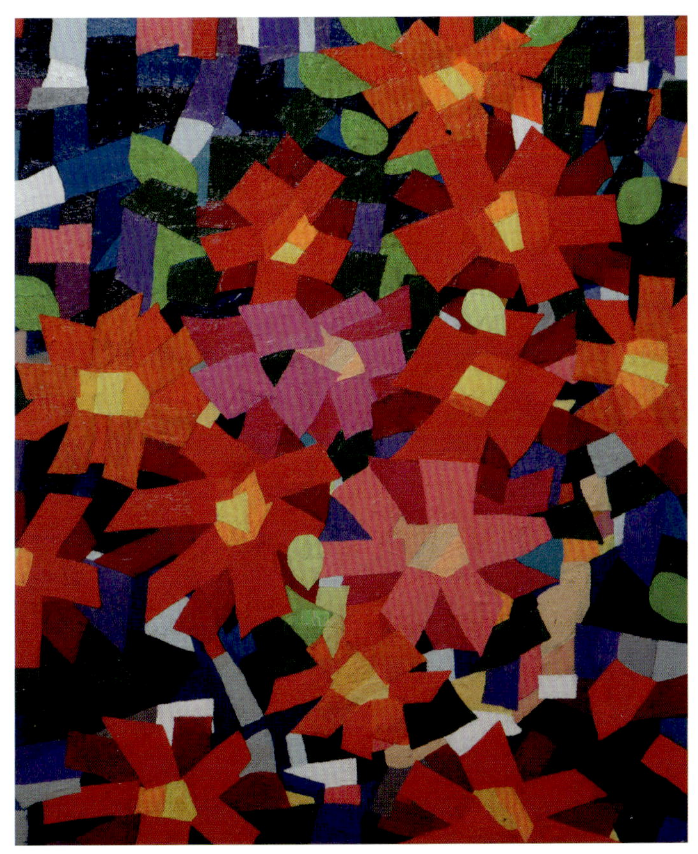

Indoor Flowers
室内的鲜花
2020, Oil on canvas, 50 x 40 cm
2020.006

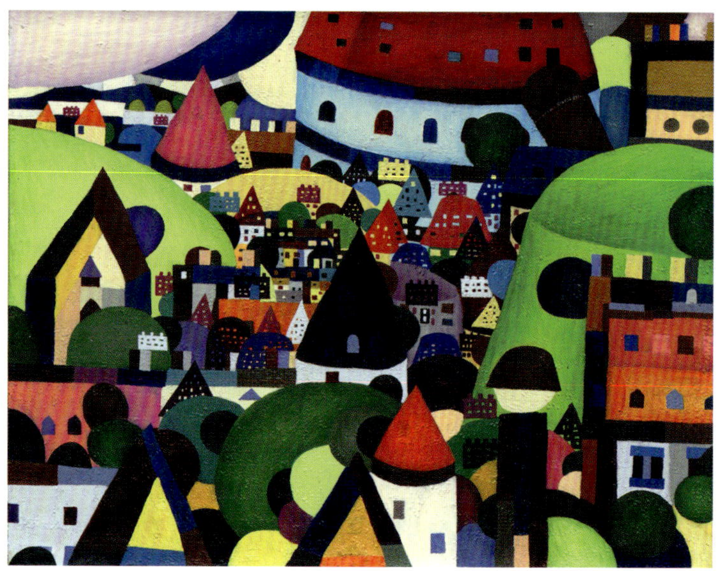

Memories and Time
回忆 时间
2020, Oil on canvas, 40 x 50 cm
2020.007

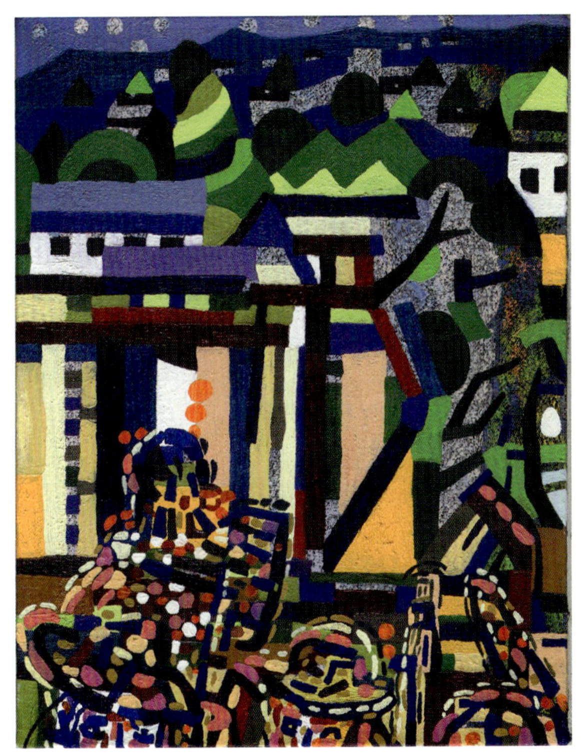

Dongxi Kindergarten
东溪幼儿园
2020, Oil on canvas, 50 x 40 cm
2020.009

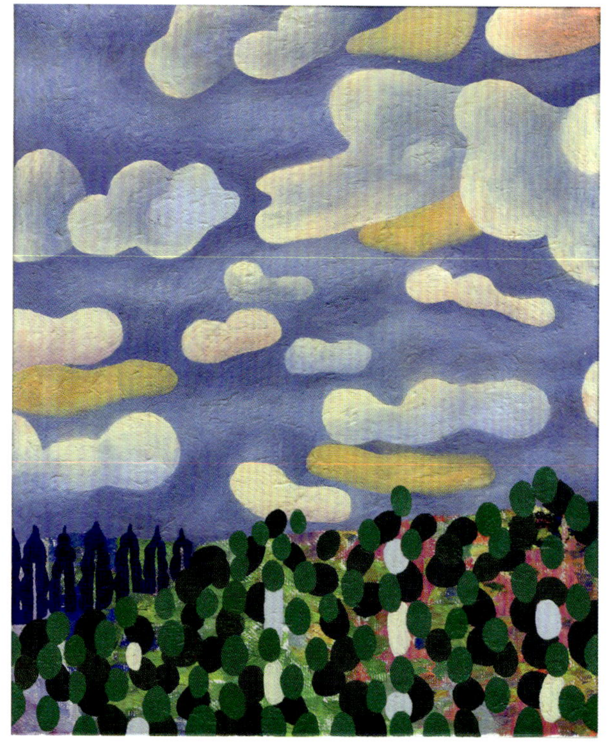

Happy Clouds
快乐的云朵
2020, Oil on canvas, 35 x 45 cm
2020.010

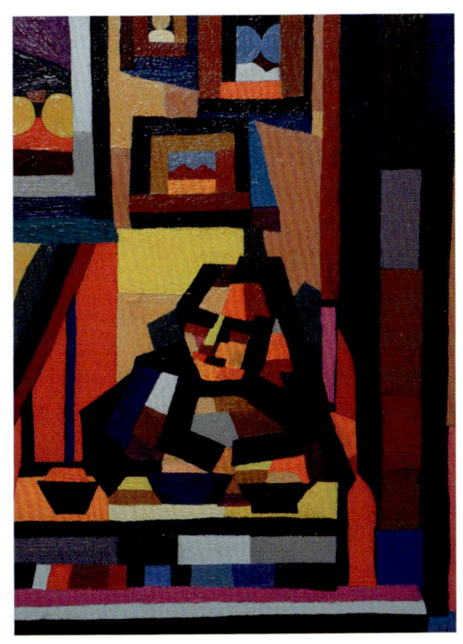

A Fast-Food Restaurant in Chengdu
成都一家快餐店
2020, Oil on canvas, 35 x 25 cm
2020.011

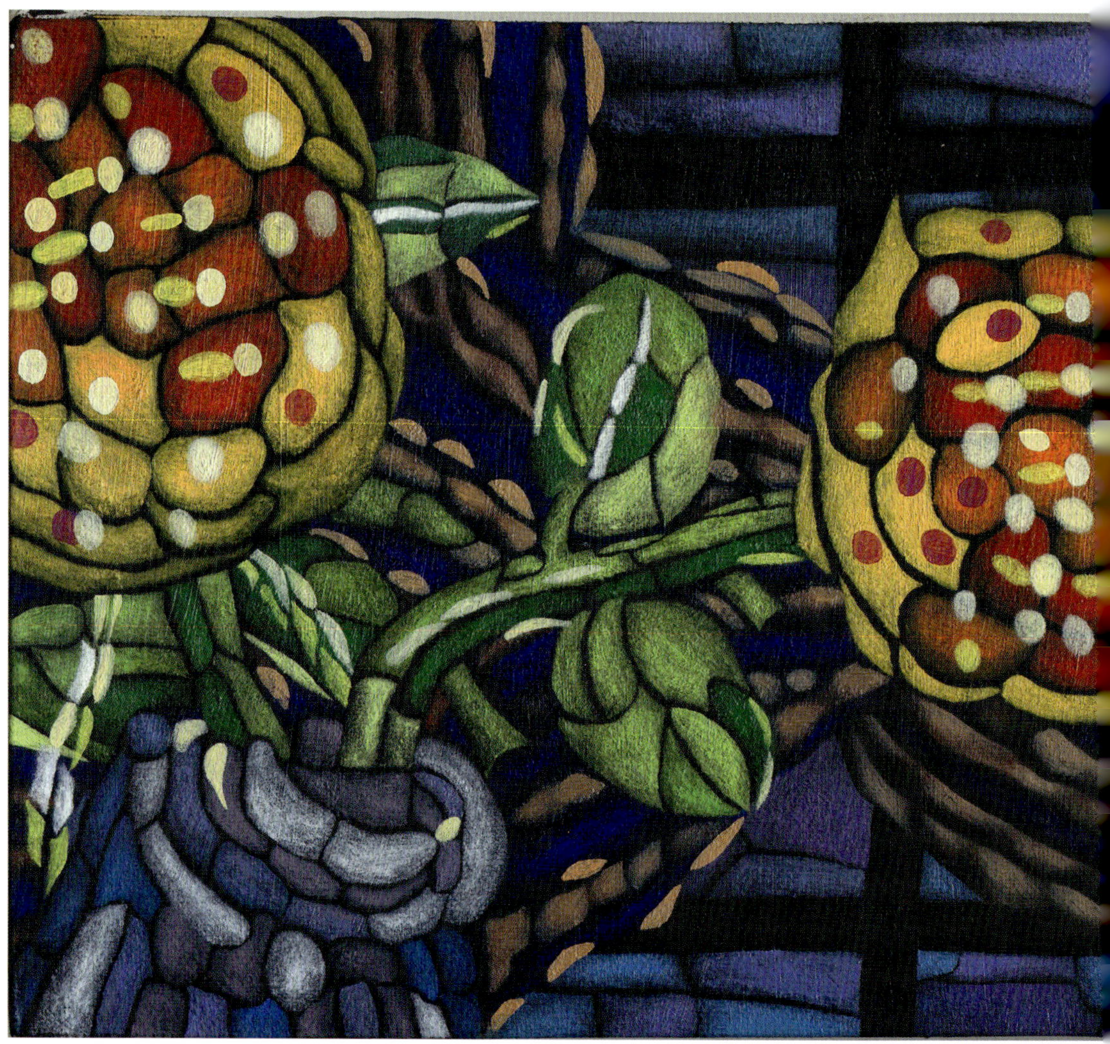

Vase and Flowers
瓶花
2020, Oil on canvas, 40 x 50 cm
2020.012

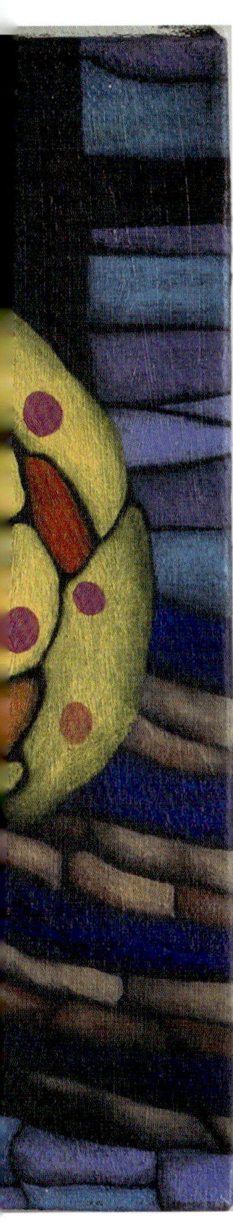

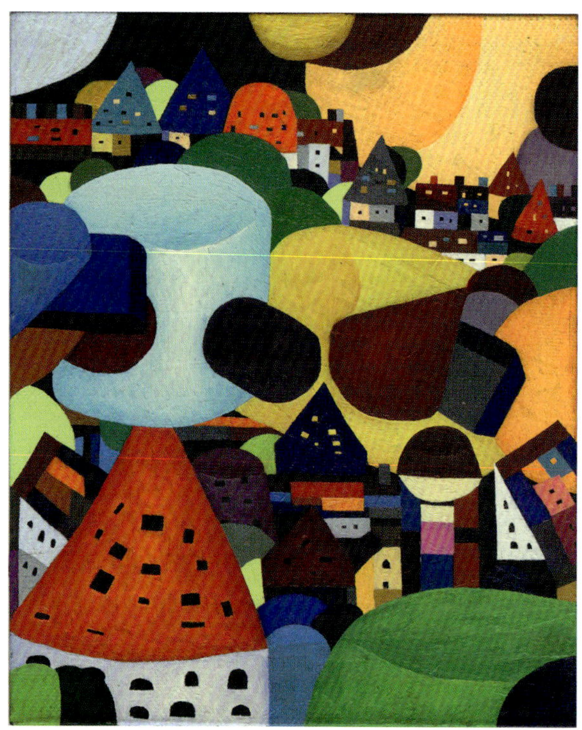

European Impressions No. 3
欧洲印象 3
2020, Oil on canvas, 40 x 30 cm
2020.013

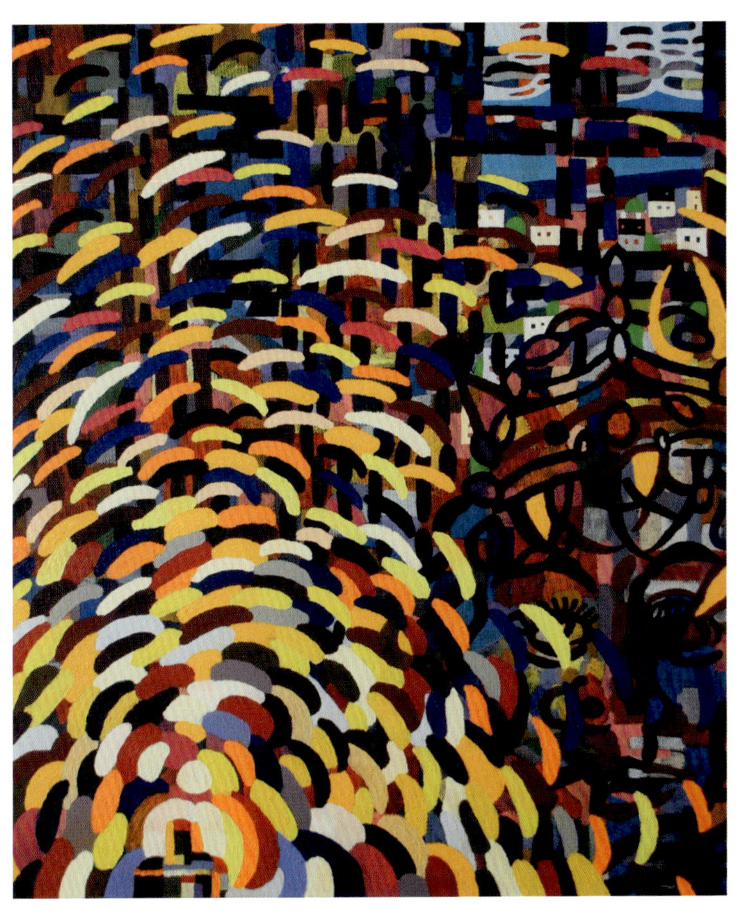

A Weaver
纺织姑娘
2020, Oil on canvas, 60 x 50 cm
2020.015

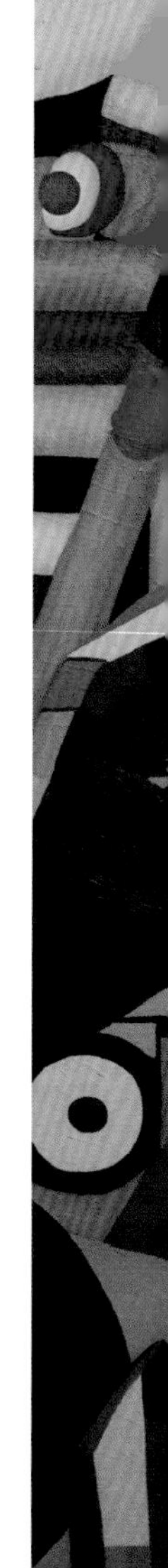

Medieval European Battlefields
欧洲中世纪战场
2020, Oil on canvas, 100 x 120 cm
2020.014

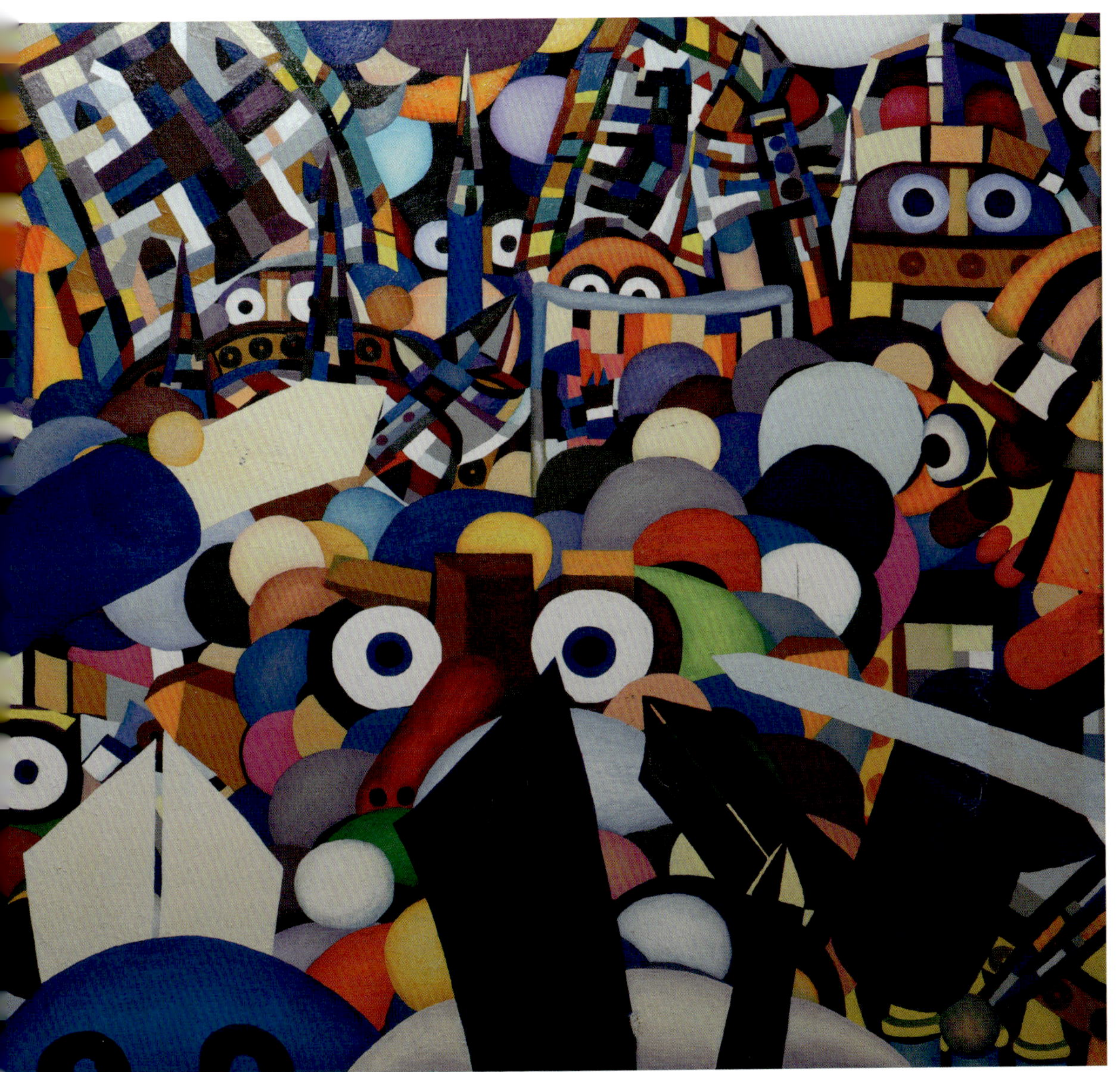

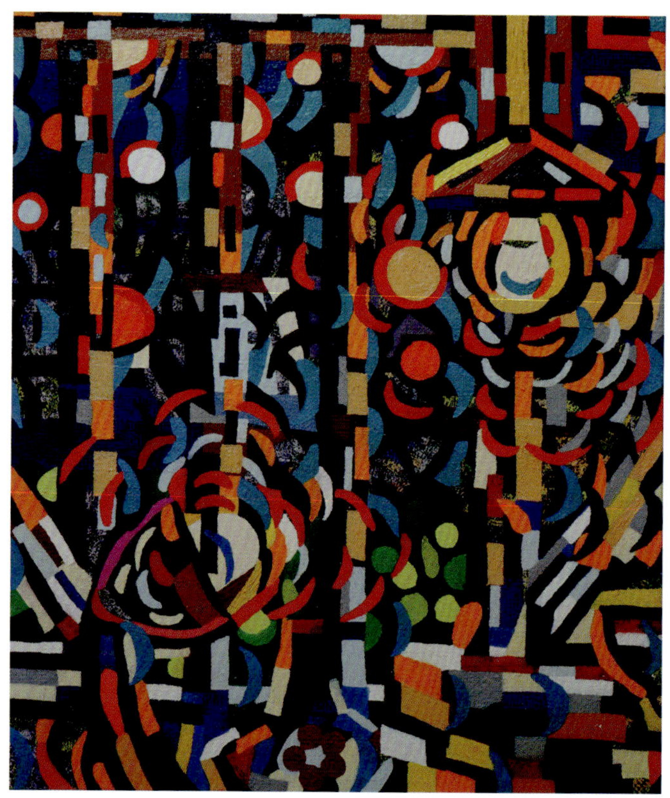

Lights at a Dongxi Farm
东溪农场的灯光
2021, Oil on canvas, 55 x 45 cm
2021.001

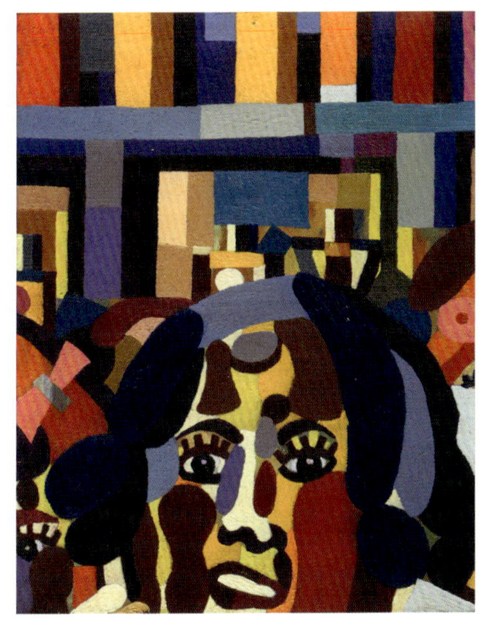

Cosmetics Store
化妆品店
2021, Oil on canvas, 40 x 30 cm
2021.002

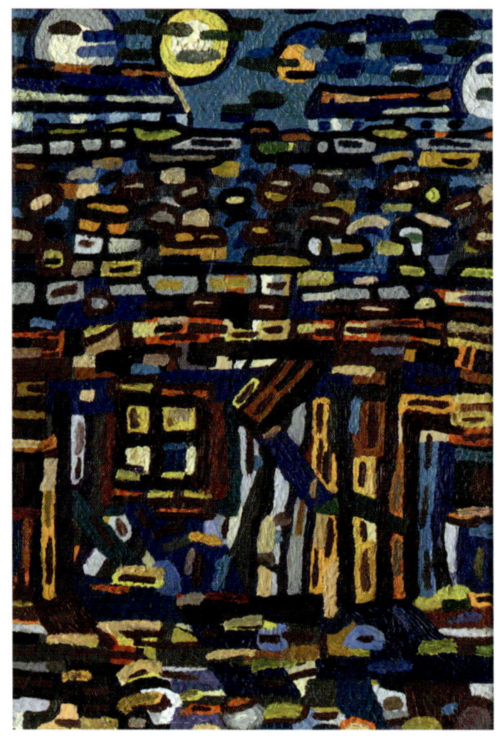

Dongxi Old House
东溪老房子
2021, Oil on canvas, 30 x 20 cm
2021.004

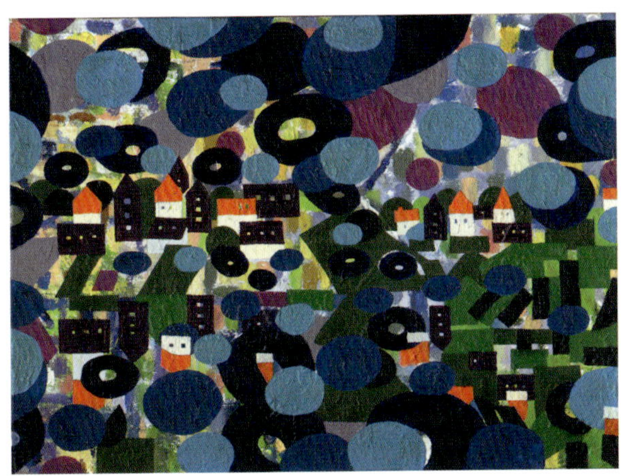

After a Painting by Isaac Levitan
临列维坦画作.湖
2021, Oil on canvas, 30 x 40 cm
2021.005

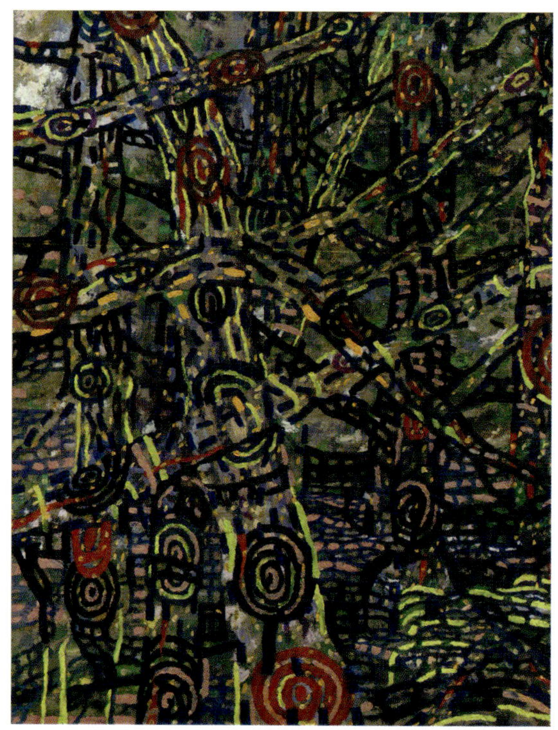

Tree Trunks
树干
2021, Oil on canvas, 40 x 30 cm
2021.006

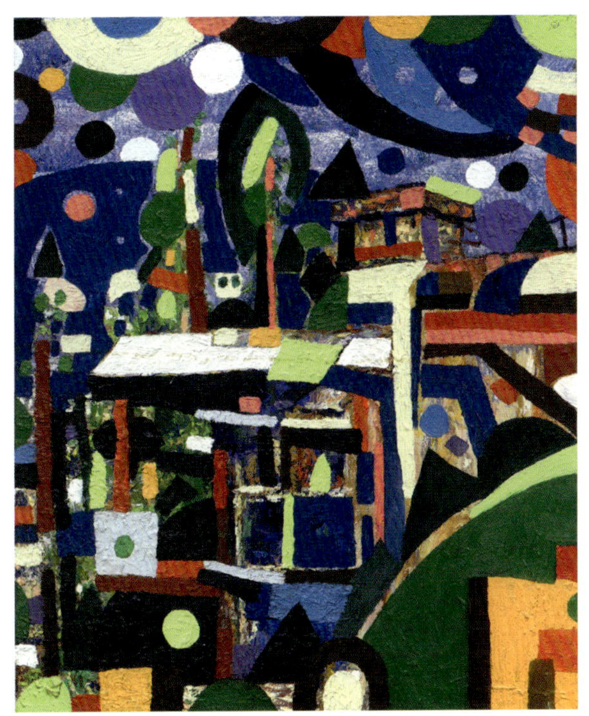

Building in the Distance
远处的筒子楼
2021, Oil on canvas, 47 x 37 cm
2021.007

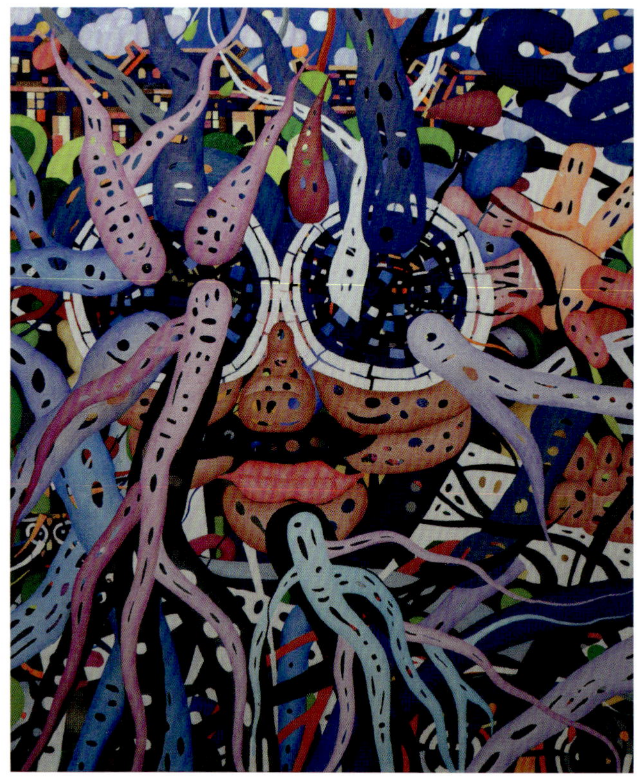

The Time-Travelling Warrior
穿越的武士
2021, Oil on canvas, 90 x 73 cm
2021.008

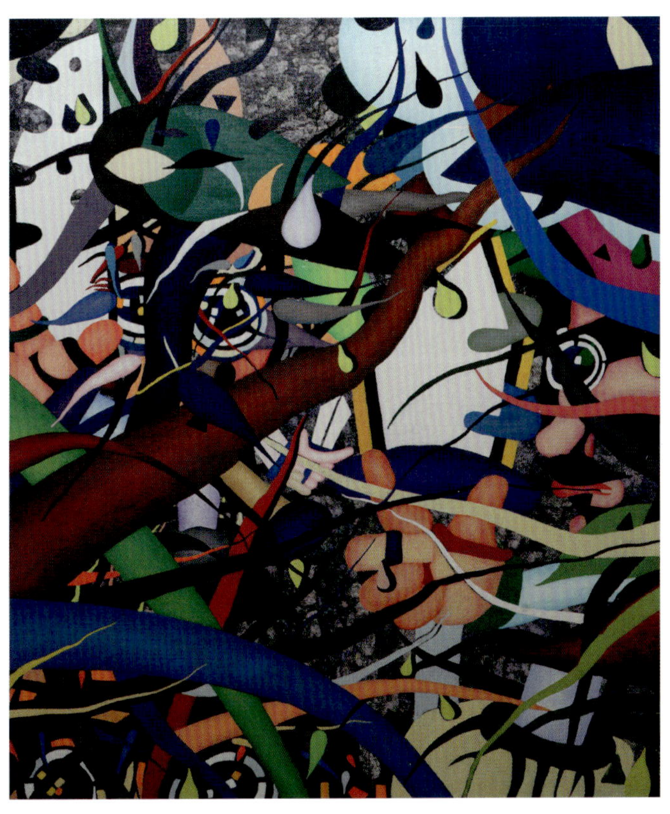

The Time-Travelling Warrior II
穿越的武士 **II**
2021, Oil on canvas, 110 x 90 cm
2021.009

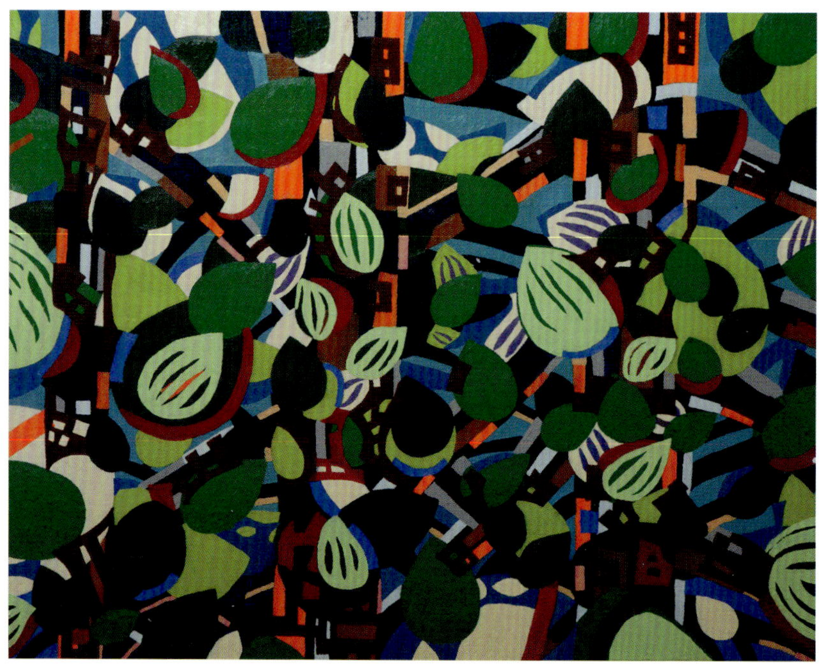

Summer Leaves
夏天的树叶
2021, Oil on canvas, 73 x 90 cm
2021.010

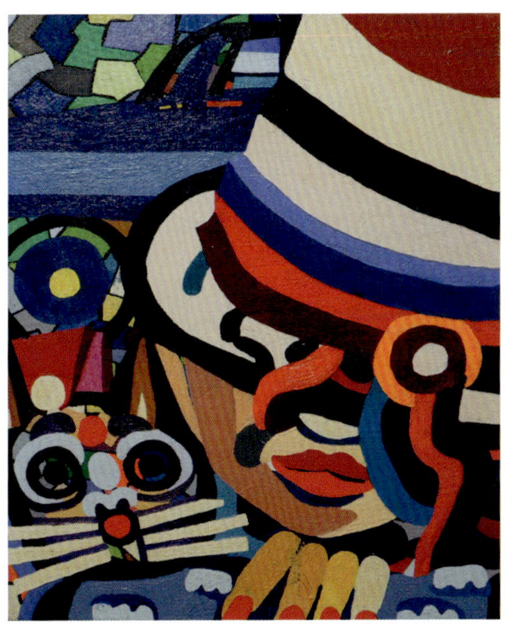

A Girl Holding a Kitten
抱小猫的女孩
2021, Oil on canvas, 45 x 35 cm
2021.012

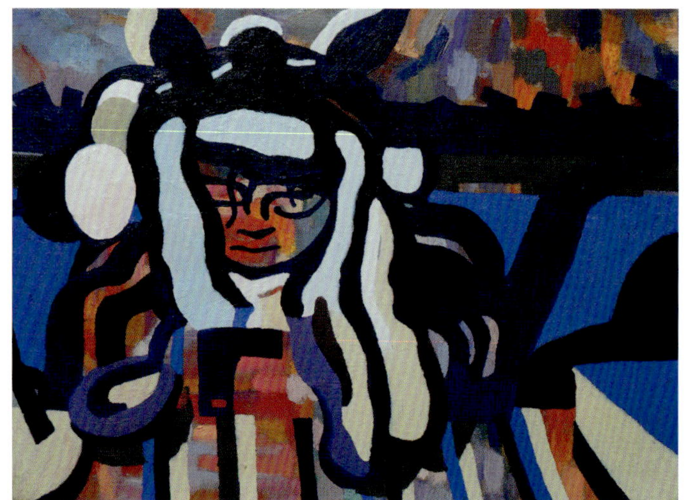

Hawker
小贩
2021, Oil on canvas, 30 x 40 cm
2021.013

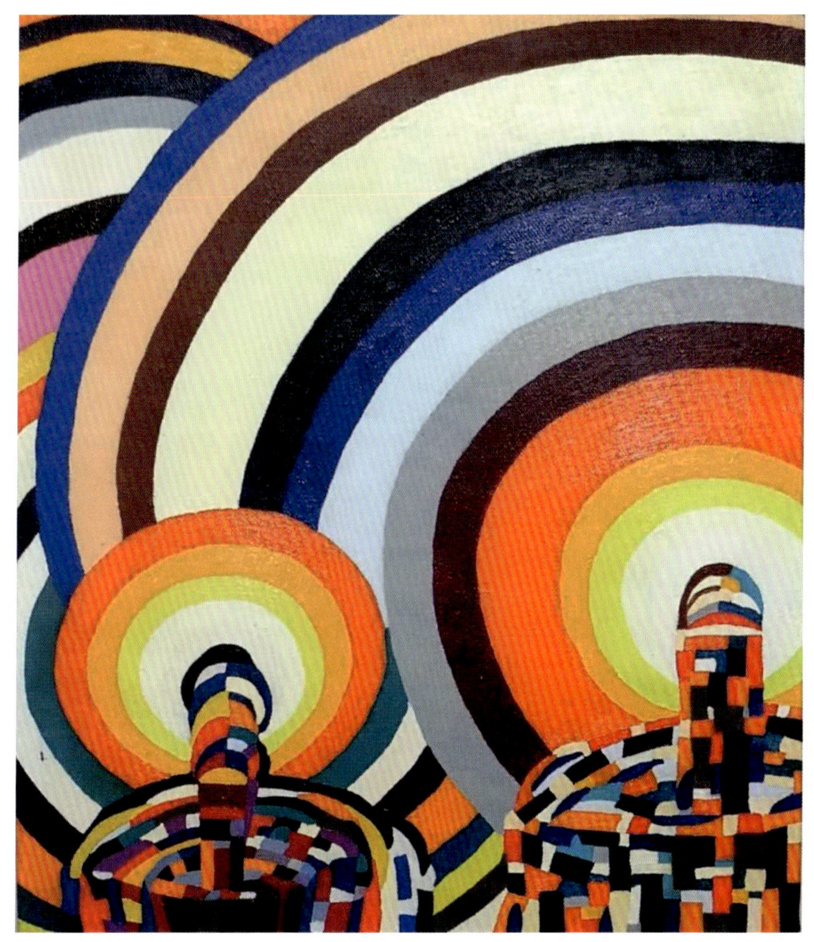

Candlelight
烛光
2021, Oil on canvas, 55 x 45 cm
2021.014

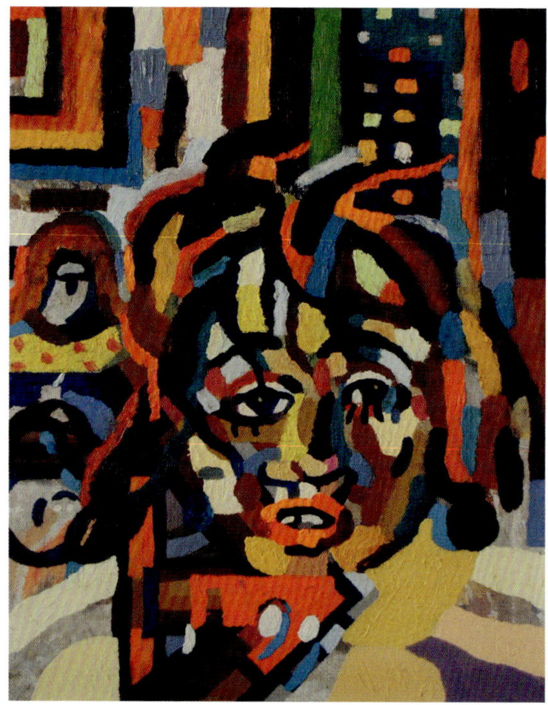

Gaze
凝视
2021, Oil on canvas, 30 x 40 cm
2021.015

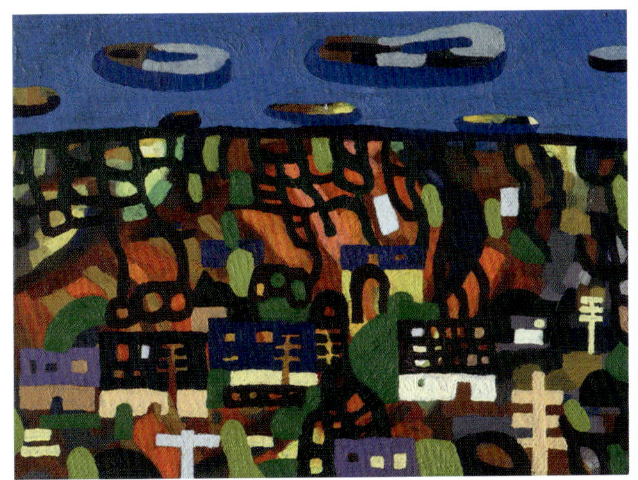

Mountain
山上
2022, Oil on canvas, 40 x 30 cm
2022.001

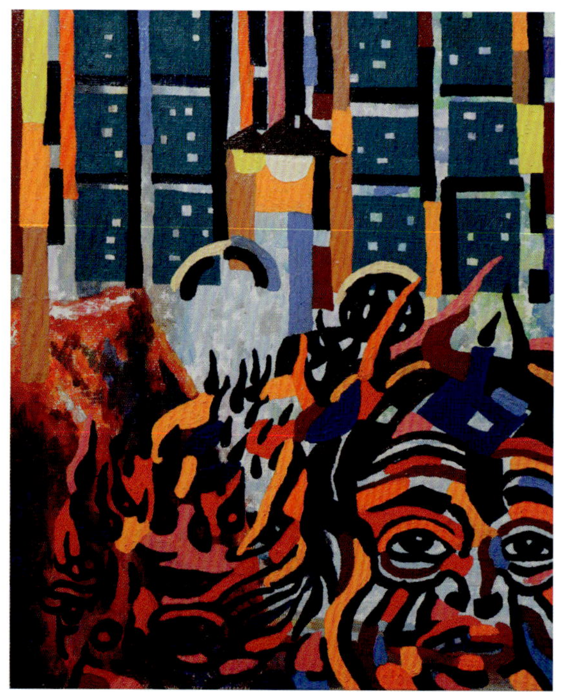

Mental Hospital Room
精神病院的房间
2022, Oil on canvas, 47 x 37 cm
2022.002

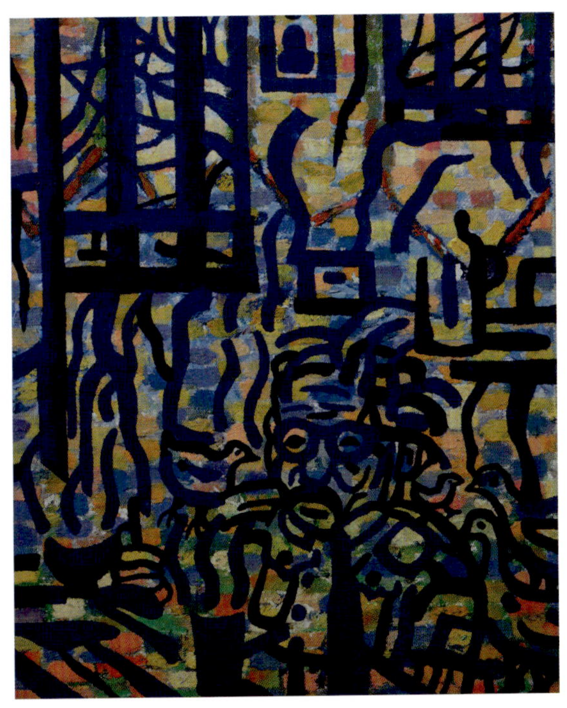

Downtrodden Father
落魄的父亲
2022, Oil on canvas, 47 x 37 cm
2022.003

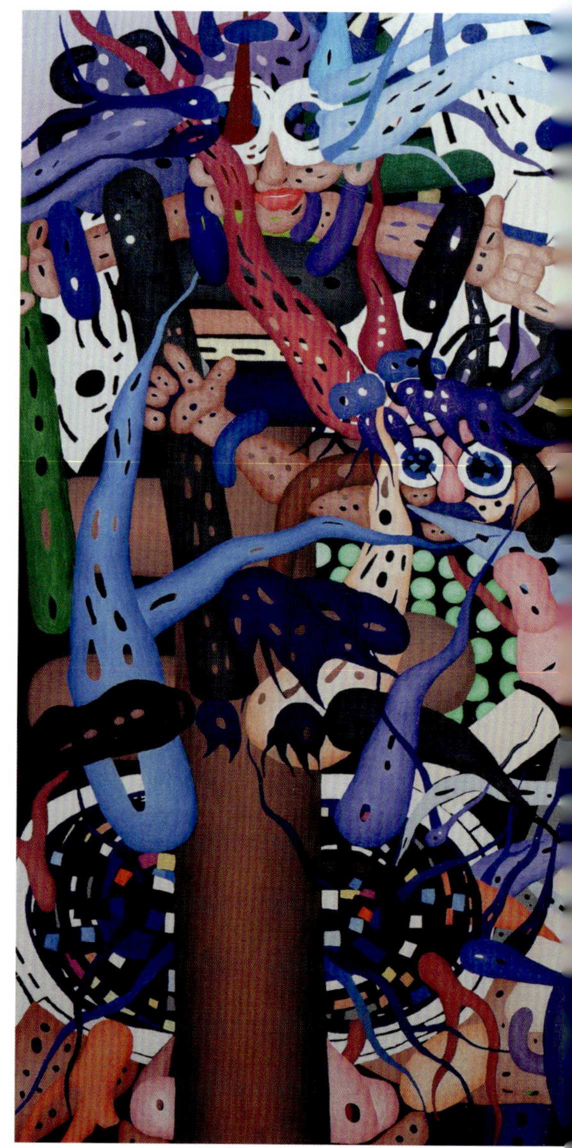

Warrior Entering the Palace
进入宫殿的武士
2022, Oil on canvas, 100 x 150 cm
2022.004

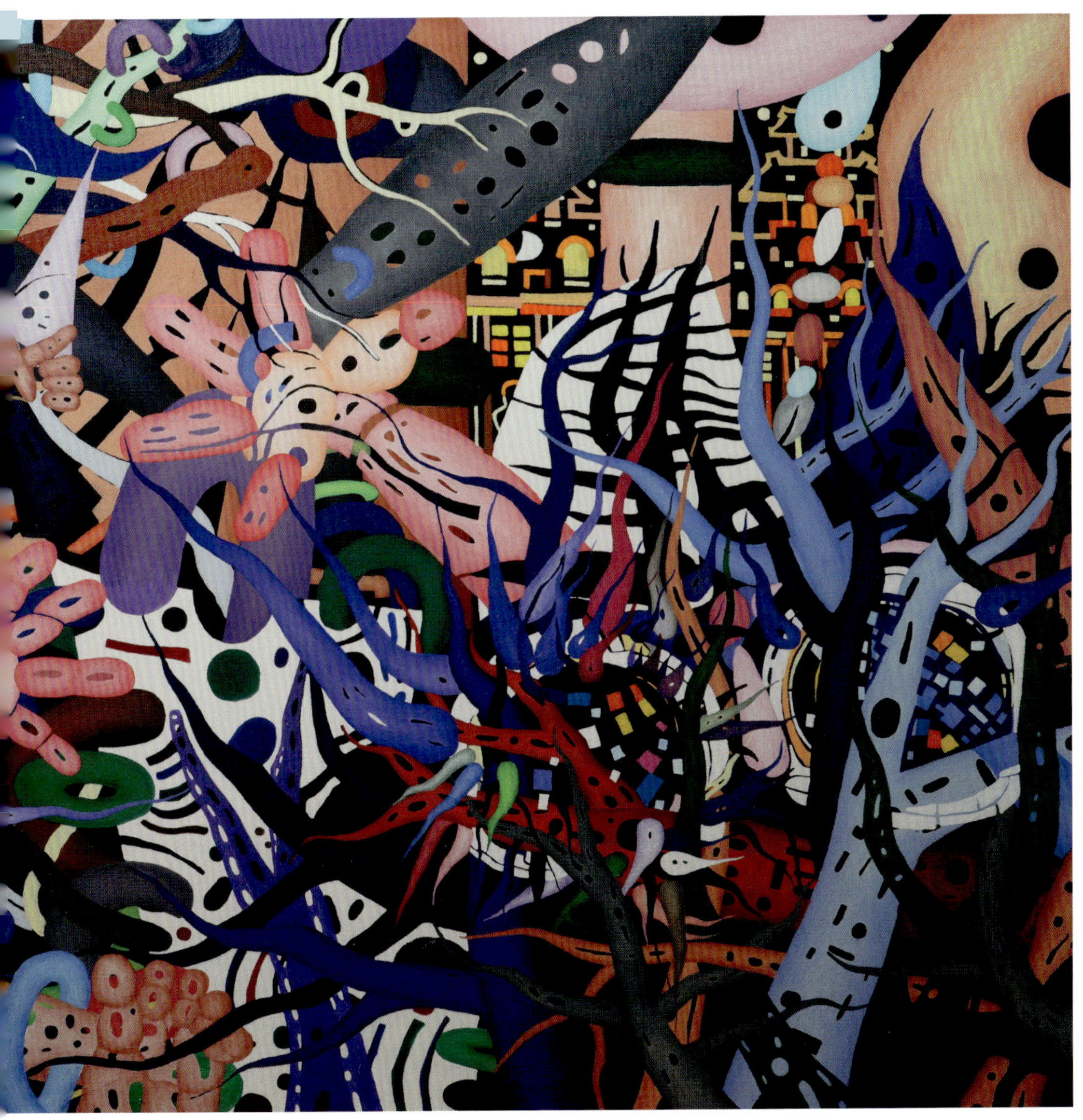

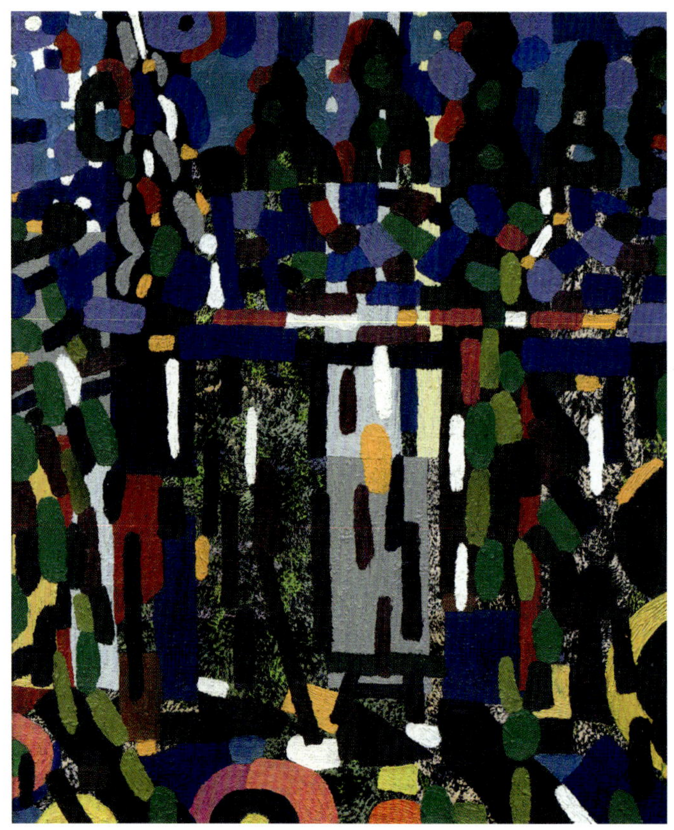

Dongxi Dingshan Township
东溪丁山乡
2022, Oil on canvas, 47 x 37 cm
2022.005

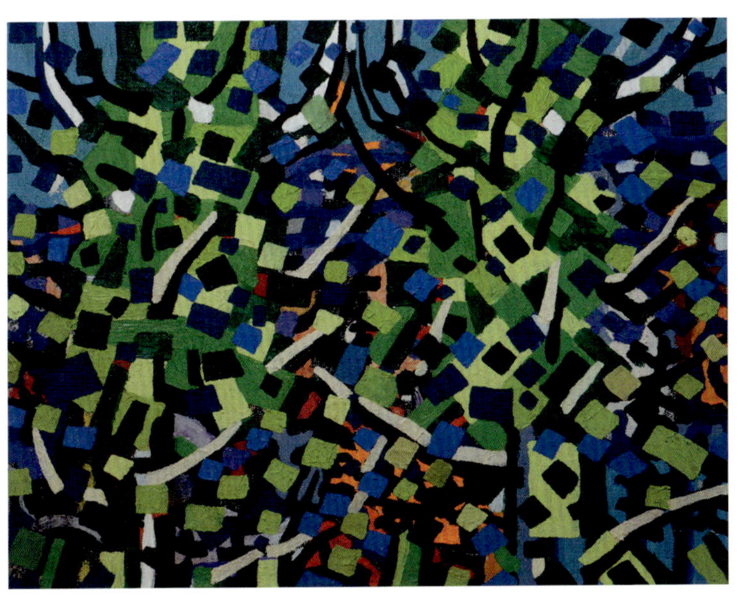

The Woods of Dingshan
丁山的树林
2022, Oil on canvas, 40 x 50 cm
2022.006

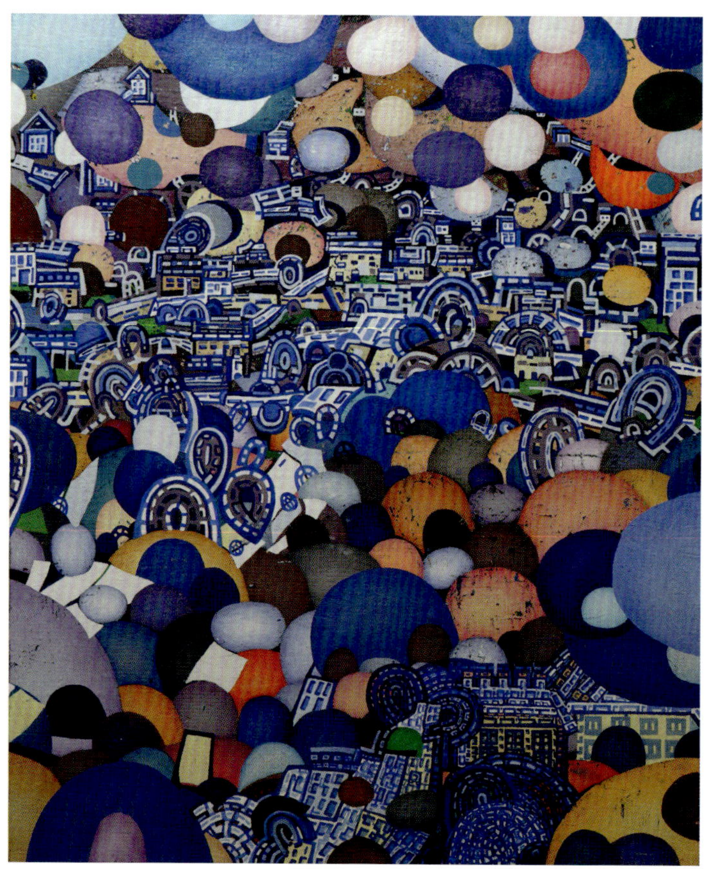

Countryside Scene
乡下小景
2022, Oil on canvas, 100 x 80 cm
2022.007

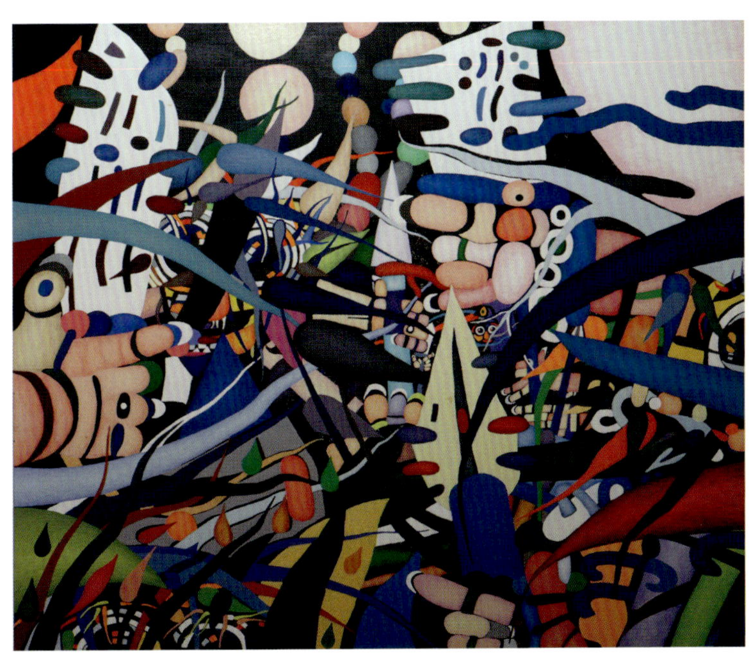

Ancient Battlefield
古战场
2022, Oil on canvas, 135 x 155 cm
2022.008

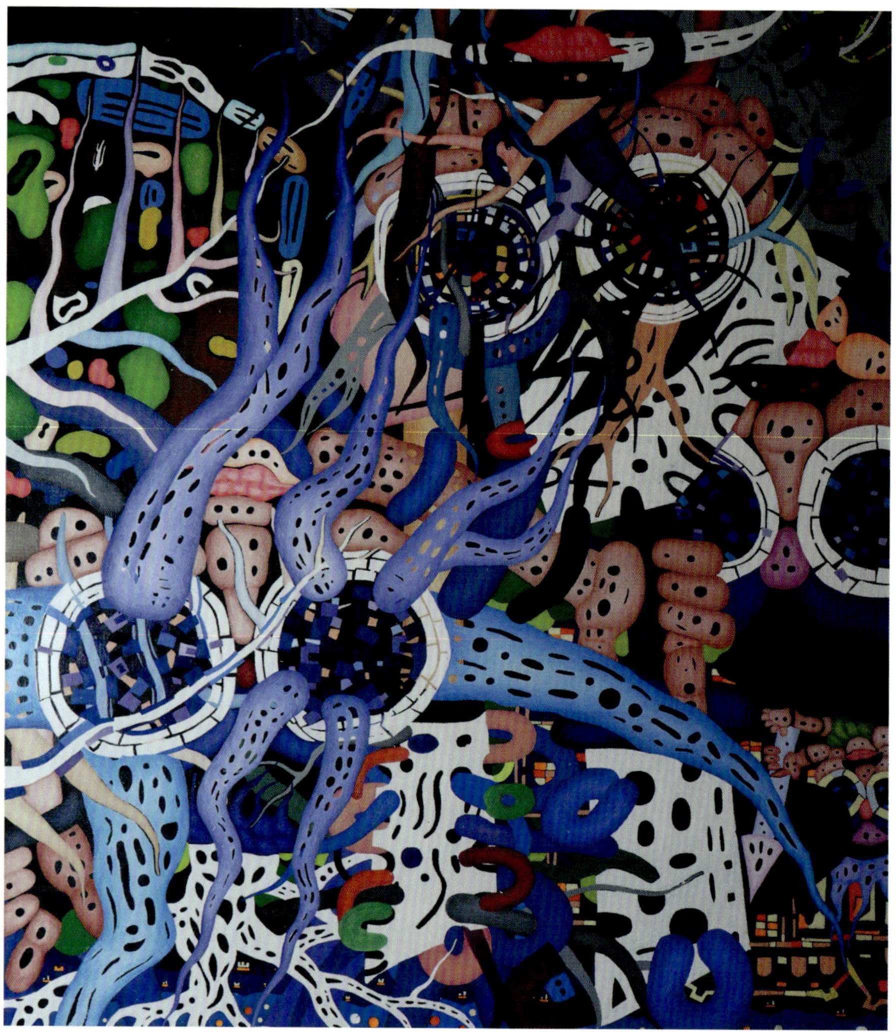

Warrior Resting in the Forest
在森林里休息的武士
2022, Oil on canvas, 120 x 140 cm
2022.009

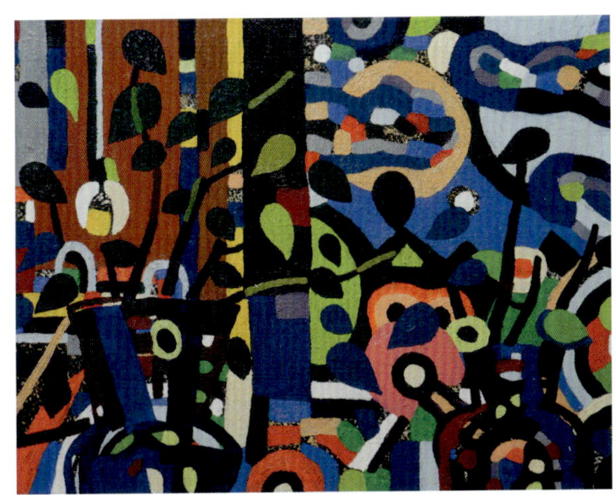

Outside the Window
窗外
2022, Oil on canvas, 40 x 50 cm
2022.011

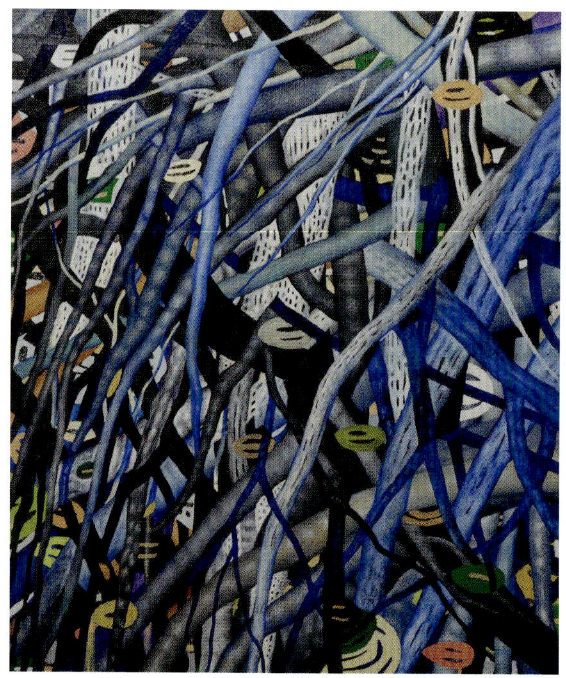

Dense Branches
茂密的树枝
2022, Oil on canvas, 55 x 45 cm
2022.012

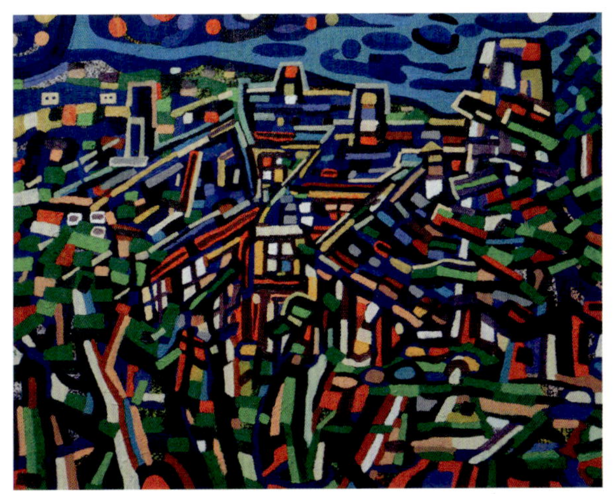

In Front of a Dongxi House
东溪住家门前
2022, Oil on canvas, 45 x 55 cm
2022.013

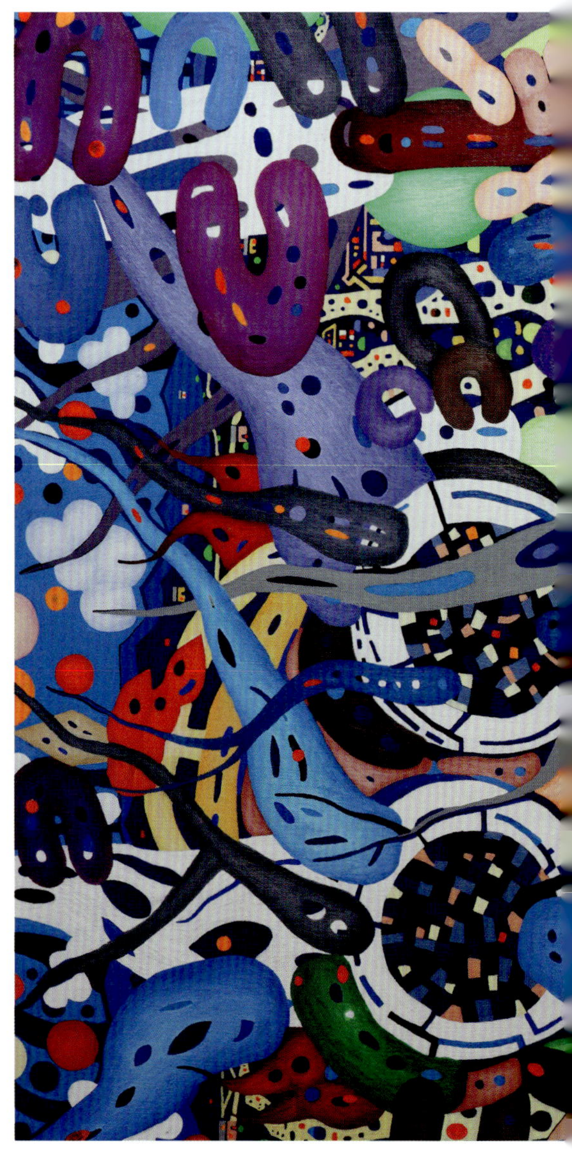

Warrior by the River
河边的武士
2023, Oil on canvas, 100 x 150 cm
2023.001

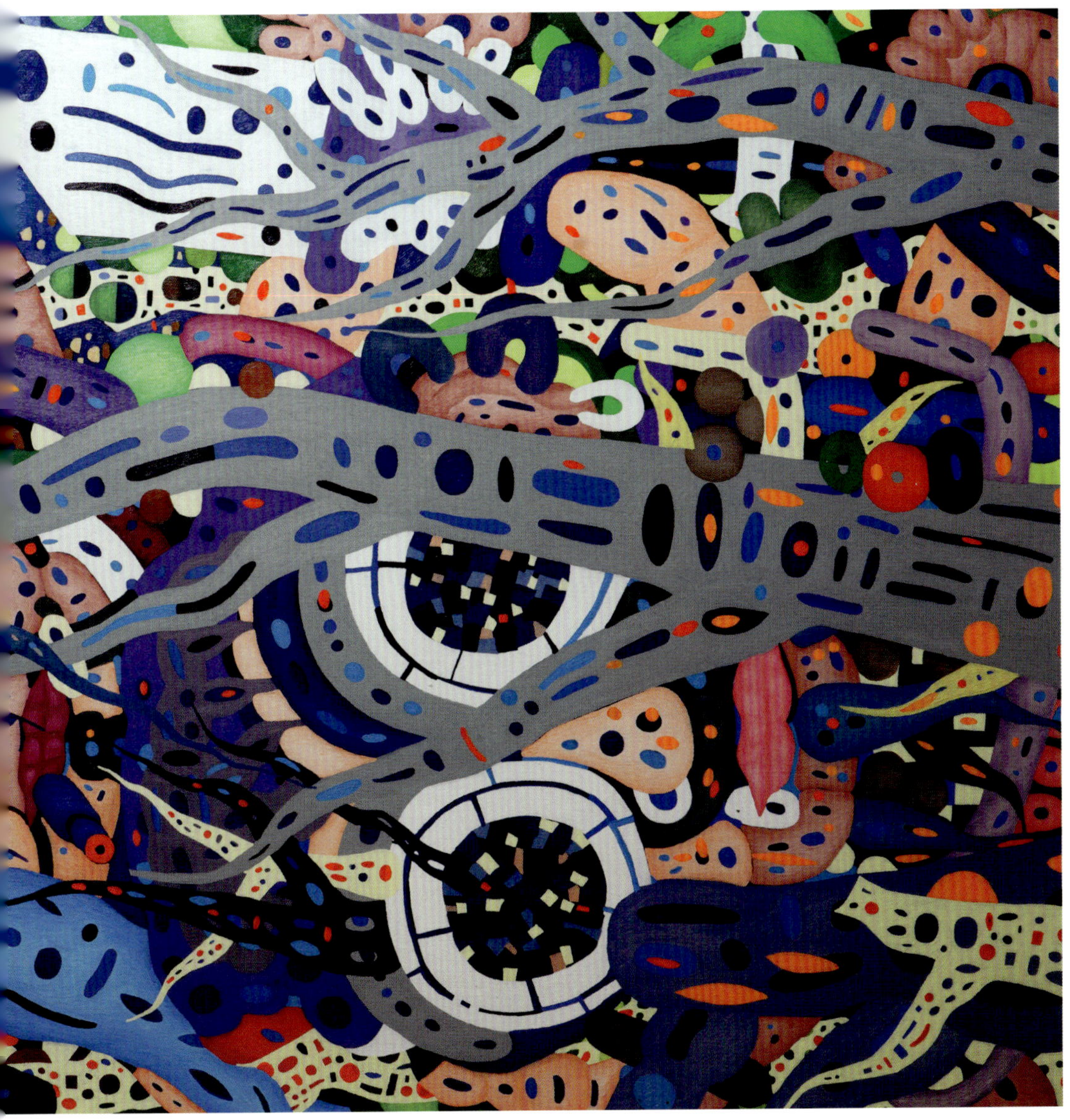

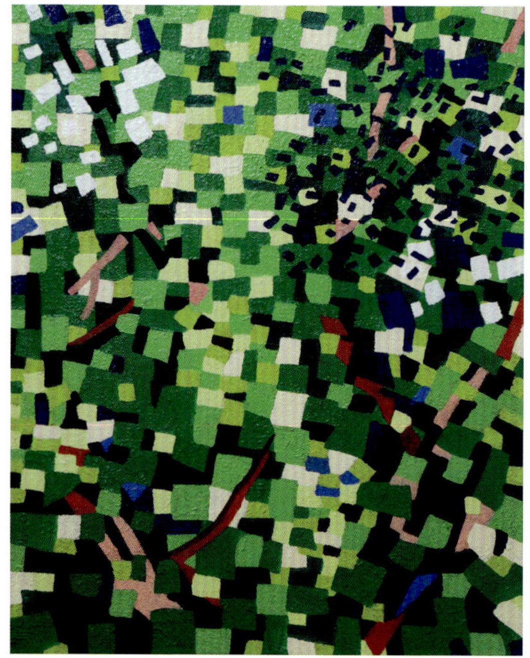

Leaves in the Sun
阳光下的树叶
2023, Oil on canvas, 45 x 35 cm
2023.002

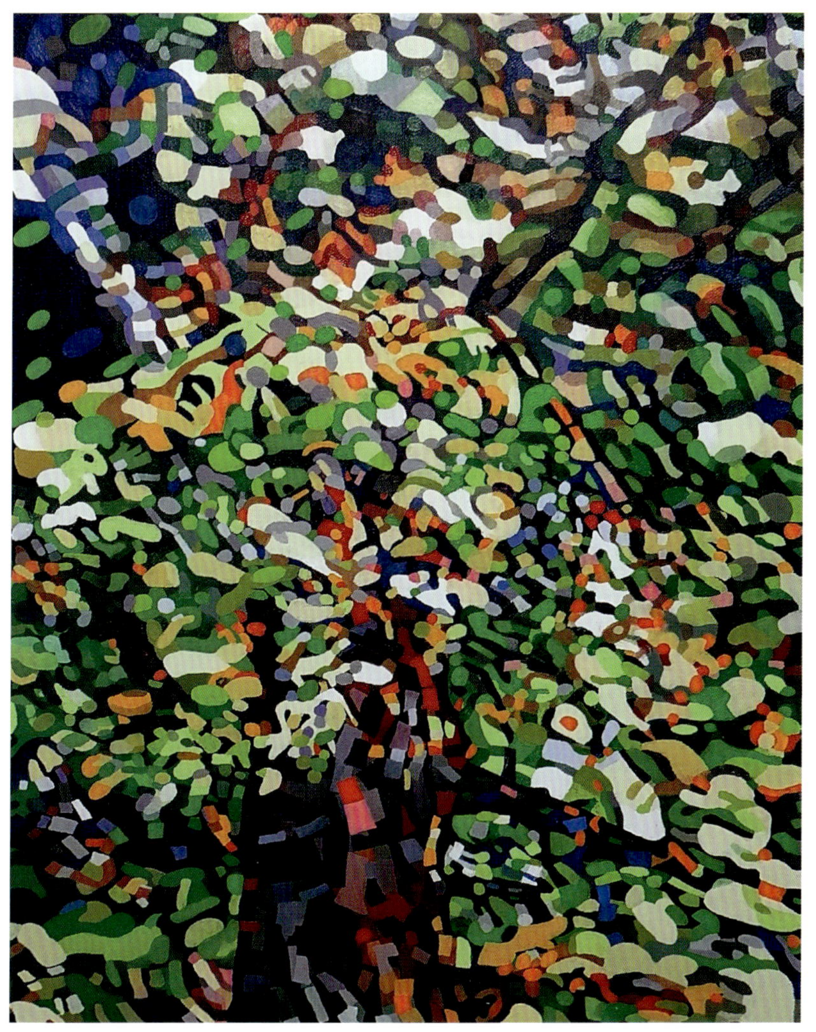

Leaves
树叶
2023, Oil on canvas, 70 x 50 cm
2023.003

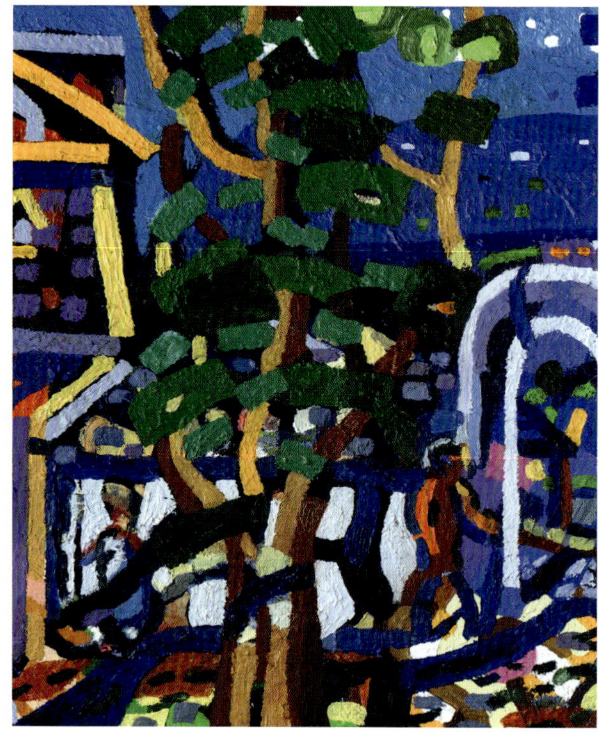

The Back Door of a Dongxi Kindergarten
东溪幼儿园的后门
2023, Oil on canvas, 30 x 40 cm
2023.005

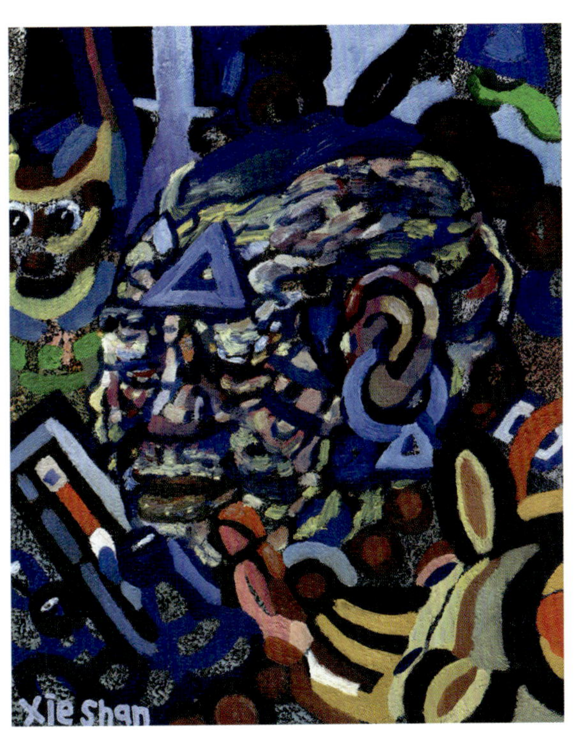

Pedestrians on the Street
街上行人
2023, Oil on canvas, 45 x 35 cm
2023.006

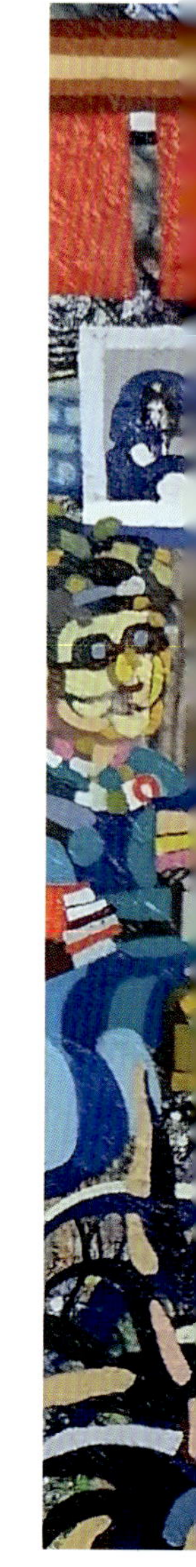

I Saw a Condemnation Meeting When I Was a Child
我小时候见到的开斗争会
2023, Oil on canvas, 60 x 50 cm
2023.007

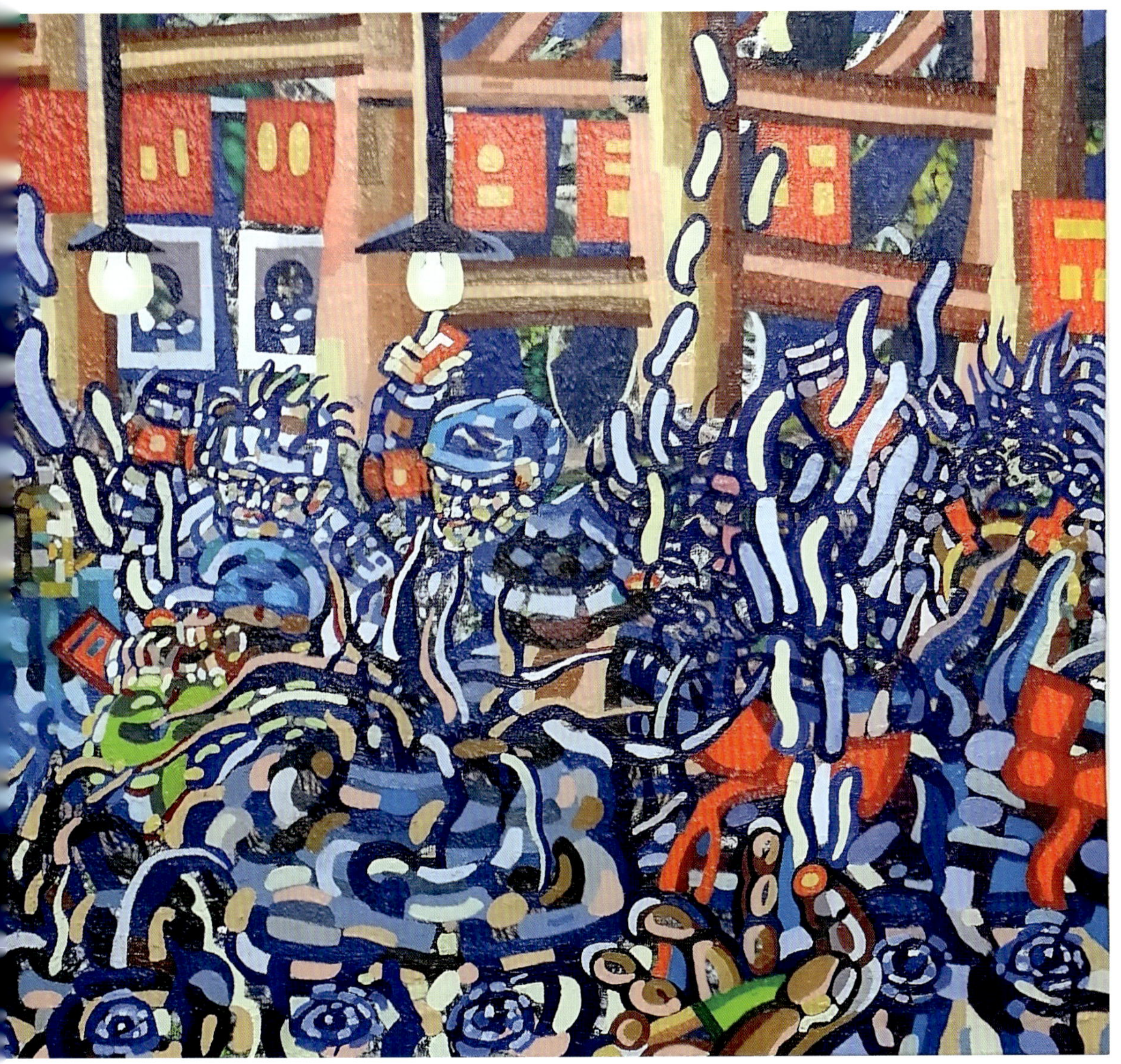

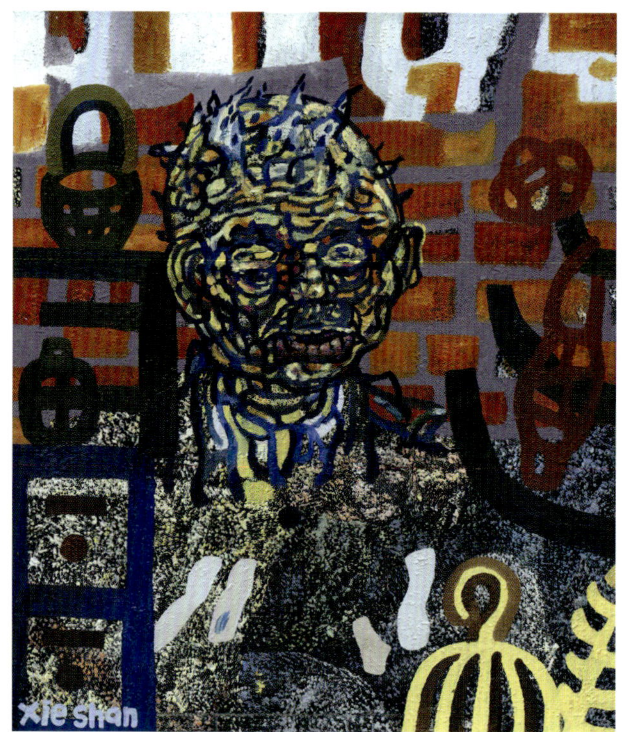

Vendor at Antique Market
古玩市场的小贩
2023, Oil on canvas, 60 x 50 cm
2023.008

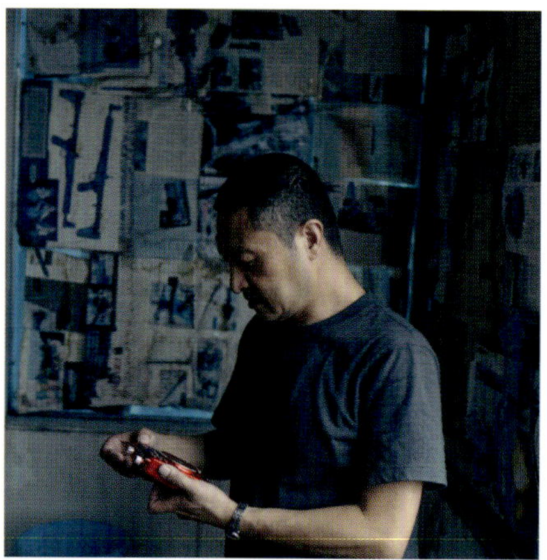

Xie Shan
Portrait

Artist Biography:

Xie Shan was born in Chongqing in 1968. He now lives in Chengdu. Xie Shan's inspiration comes primarily from memories of his hometown. He often uses dense dots or geometric brushstrokes to depict scenes from life. He developed a unique artistic style through years of self-taught practice. Although Xie Shan has no formal art education, his works exhibit the delicacy and sensitivity characteristic of trained artists. His passionate and sincere approach to art is particularly valuable in today's art world. These qualities have shaped his remarkable journey as a painter.

Solo Exhibitions:

2014
A Personal Arcadia
Nanjing Avant-Garde Contemporary Art Center

2023
The Knight of Wasteland
Beijing Tong Gallery+Projects

2023
Xie Shan - A Humble Painter
Guangzhou MOORDN Contemporary

2024
Warm Light
Shanghai BAIwork

2024
Xie Shan's Woods
Shanghai Nine PointWater Art Museum

2024
Faith in Vision
Fan Zhen & Xie Shan Dual Exhibition,
Beijing Art Center, International College
Central Academy of Fine Arts

Dedicated to my late mentor, Prof. David Alan Mellor (1948–2023)

Author's Postscript:

In 2008, during an unprecedented boom in the Chinese art market, I came to the UK with dreams of becoming a world-class art historian. By a stroke of luck, I was fortunate to be recognised by Professor David Mellor, who introduced me to a brave new world. Here, art, history, literature and music are not confined by any particular methodology. Prof. Mellor believed my skills in formal analysis and my broad knowledge base were sufficient for completing a PhD. He spent more time guiding me into his comprehensive visual culture writing environment. He once said that writing art history should be as captivating as writing a novel, with historical facts as the foundation. It was he who made me appreciate the brilliance of English literature. ***Being a Painter: The Art of Xie Shan*** is my attempt to practice Prof. Mellor's art history writing philosophy. Sadly, Prof. Mellor passed away last year. Not having his guidance and criticism during the writing of this book is my greatest regret. I hope to persevere and live up to his expectations, continuing to strive towards the ideal of the Renaissance man.

Additionally, I want to thank many teachers, colleagues, friends and family for their help and support. Professor Lv Peng has been my guide in Chinese contemporary art history. I am deeply grateful for his long-standing care and encouragement. Professor Hu Guanghua was the mentor who advised me to study art history methodology in the UK, thus changing the course of my academic career.

Furthermore, I want to thank many friends who supported my academic research: Prof. Liz James (University of Sussex), Prof. Maurizio Marinelli (University College London), Prof. Wu Hung and Prof. Eugene Wang (Harvard), Prof. Shen Kuiyi (University of California, San Diego), Prof. Fan Jingzhong, Prof. Yang Zhenyu, Prof. Kong Lingwei and Dr He Yiyang (China Academy of Art), Prof. Peng Feng and Prof. Zhu Qingsheng (Peking University), Prof. Shao Hong (Guangzhou Academy of Fine Arts), Prof. Martin Kemp (Oxford University), Prof. Chen Heng (Shanghai Normal University), Prof. Guo Liang (Shanghai University), Dr Li Xiaofei (Chinese National Academy of Arts), Dr Wu Ruoming (Nankai University), Dr Li Baoping, Dr Malcolm McNeill (SOAS), Dr Wang Tao (Art Institute of Chicago), Dr Quincy Ngan (Yale), Dr Winnie Wong (Berkeley), Dr Francesco Morena, Elena Bao (The Commercial Press), Harry Liu and Rinka Fan (Artzip), Mr Tan Zhenghui, Virginia Cimino, Ilona Albertino and many more.

Also, I want to thank my friends, Dmitry Kuleshov, Svetlana Kuleshova, Mandy Wong, Katrina Jia, Li Lin, my parents and my uncle for their unconditional support and encouragement. Finally, I would like to express my gratitude to Violet Marčenkova for her invaluable input and assistance in tackling the challenge of discussing the artist's identity as an 'other' ('d'autres'); without her, this project would have been a failure.

Joshua Gong
12th March 2024

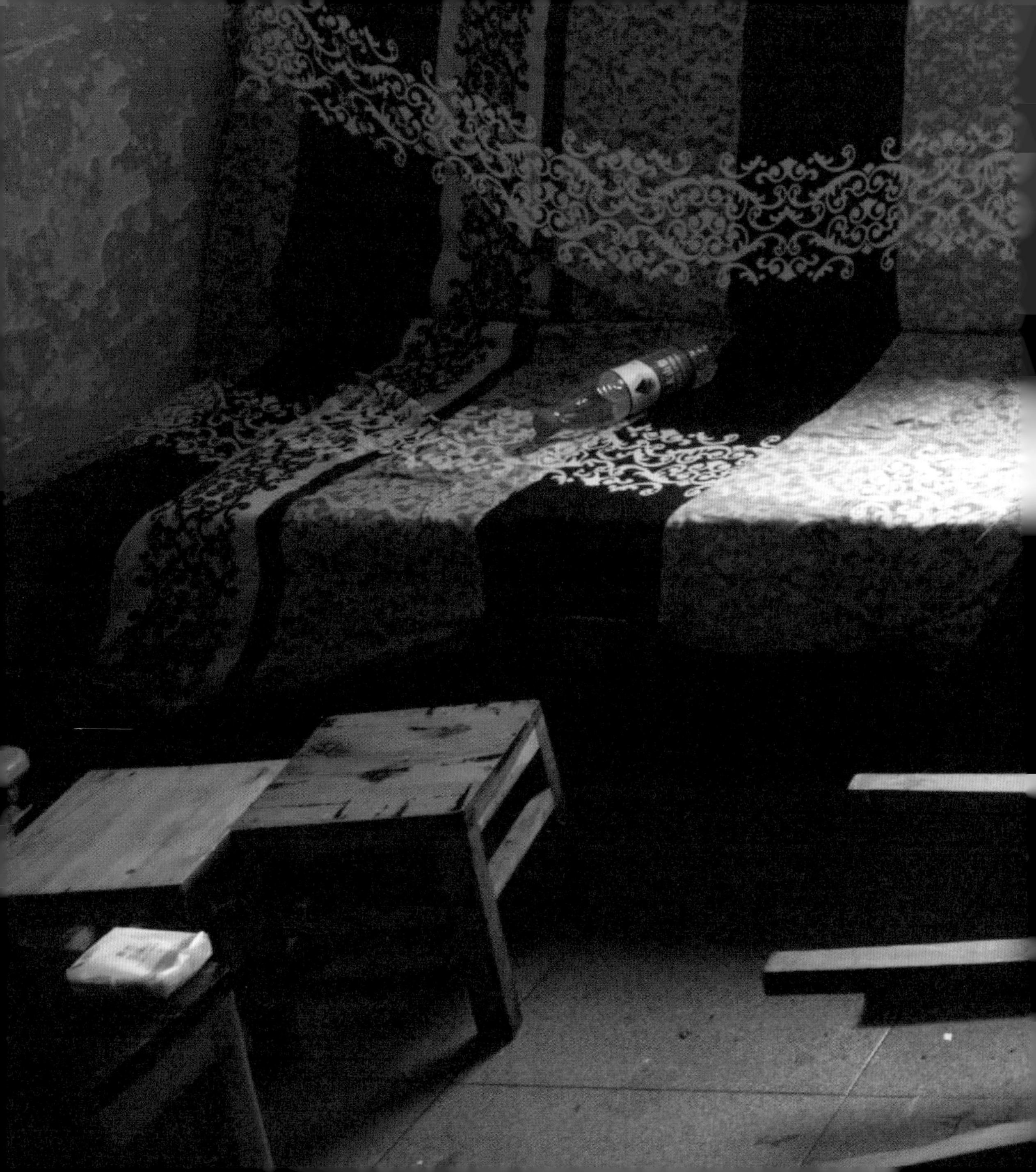